HONORS, MEDALS AND AWARDS OF THE KOREAN WAR

KEVIN R. INGRAHAM

Photography by Michael R. Parrillo

PROSPECT PRESS / KEVIN R. INGRAHAM
P.O. BOX 1911
BINGHAMTON, NEW YORK 13902-1911
UNITED STATES OF AMERICA

Printed by:
Johnson City Publishing, Inc.
Binghamton, New York 13903

1993

COPYRIGHT 1993 © KEVIN R. INGRAHAM

ISBN 0-9635795-0-9

All rights reserved. No part of this book may be reproduced or transmitted in any form or by any means, electronic or mechanical, including photocopying, recording or any information storage and retrieval system, without prior permission in writing from the author.

First edition 1993

IN MEMORIUM

SSG MARK L. ALEXANDER
7th SPECIAL FORCES GROUP (AIRBORNE)

THE BEST OF FRIENDS AND A TROOPER WHO WAS OUTSTANDING, EVEN AMONGST THIS ASSEMBLAGE OF THE FINEST SOLDIERS ANY ARMY COULD PRODUCE.

PHOTO CREDITS

Photography is by Mr. Michael Parrillo of Endwell, New York.

Other photographs and permission to use them was kindly provided by:

Argyll & Sutherland Highlanders Regimental Museum: pp122 both.

John J. Barnes: pp51 top-left. Belgian Army Historical Section: pp18.

David Cabral/Joe Shields/O.M.S.A.: pp69 top-right medal.

Duke of Cornwall's Light Infantry Museum: pp124 both.

French Army Photograph & Film Institute (E.C.P.A.): pp54; 55; 58.

Kevin R. Ingraham: pp25 top; 111; 121; 125; 141; 72.

King's Own Scottish Borderers Museum: pp123 bottom.

D.G. Kinne G.C. / A. Cunningham-Boothe: pp126. Dr P. Farrar/A. Cunningham-Boothe: pp132. James W. Lang: pp15 bottom; 63 bottom; 69 row 2; 82; 45 left; 113 top-left George Forty/United Nations Photo Library: pp62.

Gunnar Nyby/Swedish Red Cross: pp106. National Archives of Canada: pp8; 12.

Netherlands Army Historical Service (S.M.G.L.): pp87; 88; 89; 90.

Netherlands Society of the Military Order of William: pp86.

Norwegian Armed Forces Headquarters: pp95.

Orders and Medals Society of America: pp72; 145.

Princess Patricia's Canadian Light Infantry Museum: pp25 bottom; 159.

Republic of Korea Embassy (U.S.A.): pp44; 97. Scottish United Services Museum/Stephen Wood: pp123 top. Don Tresham/Canada D.N.D.: pp1; 30; 32.

Royal 22e Regiment Museum: pp22; 27; 31. Sotheby's/David Erskine: pp33.

United Nations Photo Library: pp7; 50; 81; 101; 120. John Zabarylo: pp93 right.

James W. Lang: Front cover- top L & R; Back cover- Left top & bottom; title page.

COVER PHOTOS

FRONT: L TO R: - U.N. KOREA SERVICE MEDAL (english coinage); U.S.A. COMBAT INFANTRY BADGE; South Korea WAR SERVICE MEDAL; U.S.A. KOREA SERVICE RIBBON with assault arrowhead and the silver and bronze campaign stars. -Infantry of the French-Canadian Royal 22eme Regiment under fire (N.A.C. #PA128848) -Canadian KOREA MEDAL & U.N. KOREA SERVICE MEDAL pair, The U.N. medal is french coinage.

TITLE PAGE: -Colombian COMBAT INFANTRY BADGE (James W. Lang)

BACK: As labeled.

CONTENTS

I	UNITED NATIONS	2
II	AUSTRALIA	10
III	BELGIUM - LUXEMBOURG	16
IV	CANADA	20
V	CHINA, PEOPLE'S REPUBLIC OF	34
VI	COLOMBIA	40
VII	DENMARK	46
VIII	ETHIOPIA	48
IX	FRANCE	52
X	GREECE	60
XI	INDIA	64
XII	NEUTRAL NATIONS REPATRIATION COMMISSION	67
XIII	ITALY	68
XIV	KOREA, DEMOCRATIC PEOPLE'S REPUBLIC OF CHOSIN	70
XV	KOREA, REPUBLIC OF	74
XVI	MALAYSIA	83
XVII	NETHERLANDS	84
XVIII	NEW ZEALAND	94
XIX	NORWAY	96
XX	PHILIPPINES	100
XXI	SWEDEN	104
XXII	THAILAND	108
XXIII	TURKEY	112
XXIV	UNION OF SOUTH AFRICA	114
XXV	UNION OF SOVIET SOCIALIST REPUBLICS	117
XXVI	UNITED KINGDOM OF GREAT BRITIAN	118
XXVII	UNITED STATES OF AMERICA	134

ACKNOWLEDGEMENTS

I owe much gratitude to all those who so kindly fielded my questions and badgering and who offered advice; without whose help this project would not have been possible. Whether it was a simple question and reply, the loan of material or putting up with barrages of questions and queries, my sincerest thanks to all who supported this effort. Their numbers grew too large to thank individually and I wish no offense by omission. Now I hadn't intended to single out any of the individuals who helped make this work possible. They are many and I am indebted indeed, but Jeff Floyd, current president of the Orders and Medals Society of America, especially earned this "Mention in Dispatches".

ORDERS AND MEDALS SOCIETY OF AMERICA

To those who are not yet members of this fine organisation, I cannot strongly enough urge you to join. Along with the knowledge gained, signing up in this society can be very beneficial to the enjoyment and satisfaction of our hobby. For current information regarding membership, send a S.A.S.E or I.R.C. to:

>SECRETARY, O.M.S.A.
>P.O. BOX 484
>GLASSBORO, NEW JERSEY 08028
>U.S.A.

Members receive the Journal ten times a year and an annual national convention is held each August in different parts of the country.

INTRODUCTION

This book is intended to illuminate one aspect of the history of the Korean War, the commemoration of deeds and service by the award of medals and decorations to those who served. This is an attempt to place in one source as much as possible about Korean War medals. The sources used vary widely and often conflict but every effort has been made to ensure accuracy. Much remains to be brought to light or clarified, much of which may be readily available to others. It is hoped that readers with corrections or new information will share it so that future editions will be more useful to all of us. Any errors are, of course, my own. Please note that the medal photographs are not to scale, as the plates contain a mix of actual medals, photos of medals and drawings.

Another purpose of this book is to raise awareness of the contributions and sacrifices of the small allied contingents. Some 40,000 non American/Korean troops served in Korea, about half of whom were British Commonwealth. These contributions are not to be taken lightly. The valor and determination of the allied troops often had results out of proportion to their numbers. While several nations had an interest in 'holding the line' against communism, others sent troops out of a sense of solidarity in response to aggression. After all, in what manner would a North Korean victory have threatened Colombia in 1950? Or consider Greece who by 1950 had been fighting on her territory for ten years. This included three years of nazi occupation and a brutal civil war. With borders on a hostile soviet bloc to defend, Greece would still help fight for another small nation on the far side of the globe. Ethiopia had bitter memories of being ravaged by Italy while the League of Nations did nothing. The Philippines could ill spare troops from their war with communist guerrillas at home but still sent battalions to Korea. The allied forces were, in relative terms, major military and financial efforts for most of the nations concerned and were not 'minor'.

The symbolic and practical value of a multi national response to aggression was displayed again in 1990 when another dictator invaded his southern neighbor.

D.N.D. photo via Don Tresham

U.N. KOREA MEDAL - English coinage.

These photos are the prints that accompanied the original press release announcing the authorization of this medal by the Canadian government.

UNITED NATIONS - KOREA MEDAL

The UNITED NATIONS KOREA MEDAL was authorized by the United Nations. It is awarded by the nations which contributed to the military effort to protect the fledgling Republic of Korea from communist aggression.

After a proposal from the Philippine delegation, the U.N. authorized a medal on December 12, 1950 in accordance with Resolution 483(V). The resulting medal was authorized by the Secretary-General of the U.N. on September 25, 1951.

Award criteria were thirty days in the Korea area of operations between June 27, 1950 to July 27, 1954, inclusive. One day assigned to an active unit or one air sortie was required of United Kingdom and Commonwealth personnel. Exceptions to the terminal dates are the Netherlands whose closing date was January 1, 1955 and Sweden and Thailand who closed on July 27, 1955. These dates do not always coincide with those specified for the national issue campaign medals.

Awards were made to U.N. personnel who served in or over Korea or on nearby seas operating in direct support of U.N. operations. No restrictions were made on nationality, rank or gender but awards were subject to the approval by the national governments concerned. Awards were to members of armed forces of U.N. member states who met the above criteria. Service in Japan and Okinawa in support of operations qualified. Also eligible were civilians in specially approved categories which directly supported U.N. military operations. They had to have worn the official uniform of their organization. One day was the qualifying period as these personnel seldom qualified for their national issue campaign medals. Such categories were national chapters of the Red Cross (U.S.A., Italy, U.K., Australia, New Zealand, Sweden, Denmark), British Order of St John Ambulance Corps, Salvation Army, Young Mens' Christian Association and the Women's Voluntary Service.

The official medal is bronze alloy with the bar and suspender style copied after the British with an American type pin brooch. The intent was for the medal to be a general service medal with additional bars for subsequent U.N. operations. Miniature versions exist in several variations.

This medal was produced in ten languages at the request of the participating nations. The Philippines received the English coinage but an unofficial Tagalog version was locally made. The languages of the official issue are Amharic (Ethiopia), Dutch, English, French, Greek, Italian, Korean, Spanish, Thai and Turkish.

The majority of the original issues were made by the Administration de Monies in Paris, France. Other makers were Medallic Arts of New York City and Stabilimenti Artistide Fiorentini of Italy.

The medals were issued unnamed except to Australians, Canadians, New Zealanders and South Africans.

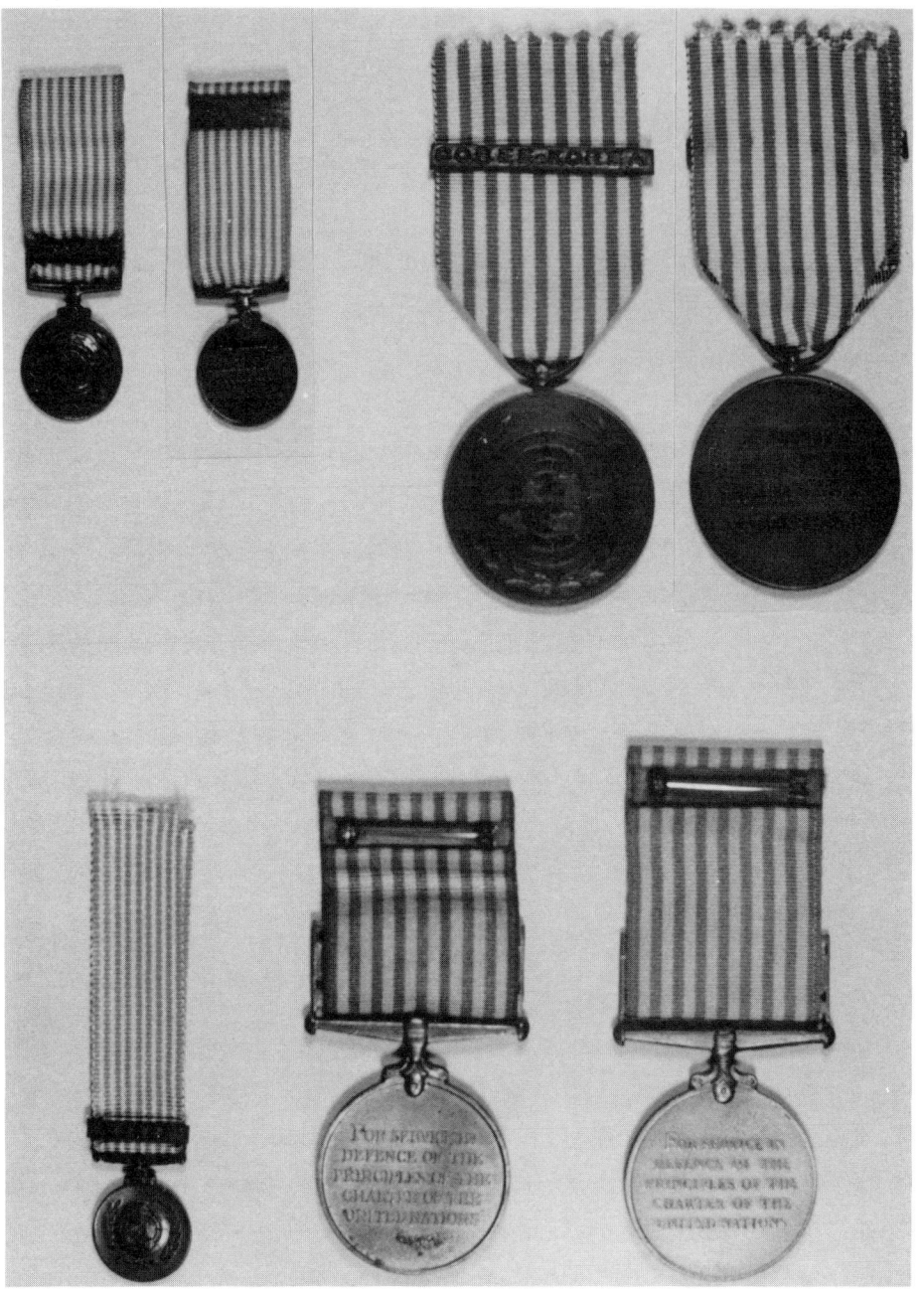

ROW 1: <u>Miniature, U.S.</u>; <u>BELGIAN</u>: Obverse, Reverse.
ROW 2: <u>Miniature, British</u>; <u>ENGLISH</u>: Reverse, second type; first type.

Notes on various coinages:

AMHARIC 5,650 struck. Ethiopian issue.
BAR: ኮሪያ.   REVERSE: ለተባበሩት፡መንግሥቶች።
                       የቃል፡ኪዳን፡መሠረቃ።
                       ግዴ፡ለግክለለ፡
                       ለተደረገ፡አገልግሎት። (4 lines)

BELGIAN Belgium originally issued the standard french coinage. The unique Belgian style was a private purchase item which later became the official issue. It has a raised rim and a ring suspension, deleting the claw and bar of the other coinages. The obverse is signed "J.DEMERET". The obverse is the same as the reverse of the Belgian Overseas Operations Medal.
BAR: COREE-KOREA   REVERSE: "POUR LA DEFENSE/DES PRINCIPES DE/
                            LA CHARTE DES/NATIONS UNIES" (4 lines)

DUTCH 5,795 struck. Netherlands issue. Some 4,000 awarded to Dutch forces. Ribbon is worn folded behind the medal in a triangular fashion.
BAR: KOREA   REVERSE: "VOOR/VERRICHTINGEN/TER VERDEDIGING DER/
                      BEGINSELEN VAN HET/HANDVEST DER/VERENIGDE
                      NATIES"   (6 lines)

ENGLISH Currently produced. Manufactured in France and the U.S.A. Lettering on reverse is smaller on the earlier samples. Commonwealth issues (except U.K.) were named. This type was issued by the following nations: AUSTRALIA, CANADA, DENMARK, INDIA, NEW ZEALAND, NORWAY, PHILIPPINES, SWEDEN, UNION OF SOUTH AFRICA, UNITED KINGDOM, UNITED STATES OF AMERICA. Over 2,700,000 struck to date.
BAR: KOREA   REVERSE: "FOR SERVICE IN/DEFENCE OF THE/PRINCIPLES
                      OF THE/CHARTER OF THE/UNITED NATIONS"
                                                          (5 lines)

FRENCH 16,851 struck. Awarded to personnel of FRANCE, BELGIUM, LUXEMBOURG, and CANADA. Canada issued English medals but French speakers could, and usually did, request issue of the French type. French-Canadian medals were named.
BAR: COREE   REVERSE: "POUR LA DEFENSE/DES PRINCIPES DE/
                      LA CHARTE DES/NATIONS UNIES"   (4 lines)

GREEK   9,000 struck. 7,050 awarded. Greece did not award a Korean
               service medal.
               BAR: KOPEA   REVERSE: "ΔΙ ΥΠΗΡΕΣΙΑΣ/ΠΡΟΣΠΡΟΑΣΠΙΣIN/ΤΩΝ
                                         ΑΡΧΩΝ ΤΟΥ/ΚΑΤΑΣΤΑΤΙΚΟΥ/ΧΑΡΤΟΥ ΤΩΝ/
                                         ΗΝΩΜΕΝΩΝ ΕΘΝΩΝ"   (6 lines)

ITALIAN   Only 131 awarded. Approved by the United Nations Command General
               Order 18 on 22 July, 1952. Approved by the Italian government on
               29 July, 1964 for the Italian Red Cross General Hospital No. 68.
               Eligibility period was 16 October, 1951 to 10 January, 1955.
               BAR: COREA   REVERSE: "PER SERVIZIO IN DIFESA DEI PRINCIPI
                                         DELLA CARTA DELLE NAZIONI UNITI"
                                                                  (5 lines)

KOREAN   1,222,000 struck. Republic of Korea issue.
               BAR: 대한민국   REVERSE: 국제련참
                                         헌장을옹호한
                                         공훈   (3 lines)

SPANISH   For Colombian issue.
               BAR: COREA   REVERSE: "PREMIO/AL SERVICIO/EN DEFENSA DE/LOS
                                         PRINCIPIOS DE/LA CARTA DE LAS/NACIONES
                                         UNIDAS"   (6 lines)

               A second spanish coinage appeared in the late 1970s. It is
               undocumented and was privately produced from an english example.
               The reverse is a literal translation from english to spanish and
               the bar reads, incorrectly, "KOREA".

TAGALOG   Unofficial Philipino coinage. Locally made by El Oro. Bar suspender
               is an integral part of the planchet. The pin brooch is marked
               "MANUFACTURED BY "EL ORO"/JOSE TUPAZ Jr/QUEZON CITY PHILIPPINES".
               BAR: KOREA   REVERSE: "SA PAGLILINGKOD/UPANG IPAGTANGGOL/ANG
                                         MGA SIMULAIN/NG SALIGANG/KASULATAN NG/
                                         MGA BANSANG/NAGKAKAISA" (7 lines)

THAI   10,648 struck. 9,785 awarded. Thailand.
   BAR: เกาหลี   REVERSE: เพื่อบริการในการ
                    ป้องกันหลักแห่งกฎบัตร
                    สหประชาชาติ   (3 lines)

TURKISH 33,696 struck. Recipients frequently replaced the ribbon with a red one.
   BAR: KORE   REVERSE: "BIRLESMIS MILLETLER/ANDLASMASI PAYOLLENNIN/
                    MUDAFAASI UERUNDA/YAFILAN HIZMET ICIN"
                                        (4 lines)

Reverse of: SPANISH; TAGALOG (El Oro made); THAI; TURKISH coinages.

U.N. #36972

Former Commander in Chief of the U.N. Forces, General Matthew B. Ridgeway, is decorated with his U.N. Korea Medal at the U.N. Headquarters on May 26, 1952.

"IN GRATEFUL REMEMBRANCE
OF THE MEN OF THE ARMED FORCES OF MEMBER STATES
WHO DIED IN KOREA
IN THE SERVICE OF THE UNITED NATIONS"

1950 - 1953

*This dedication is taken from the Memorial Plaque at the United Nations Headquarters in New York.
(N.A.C.#PA 128813)

THE KOREA MEDAL

AUSTRALIA

Australian forces were the first to join the Americans in assisting Korea in her defense. No.77 Squadron, Royal Australian Air Force, joined the U.S. Air Force in close air support missions in July, 1950.

Australia's contribution was three infantry battalions, an aircraft carrier with escorts and two air force squadrons.

Approximately 16,000 Queen's Korea Medals and 18,000 U.N. Korea Medals were awarded to Australians.

The Korea Medal awarded to Australians is the same medal awarded to the United Kingdom and New Zealand. The Australian Korea medals are distinguished from other issues by the naming. The Australian medals are impressed on the rim with the recipient's service number and name, IE: "5/9012 W.S.E. PAYTON". A prefix number with slash indicates which state the servicemember enlisted from.

1/	Queensland	4/	South Australia	7/	North Australia
2/	New South Wales	5/	West Australia	8/	Papua & New Guinea
3/	Victoria	6/	Tasmania		

Like several other nations, Australia supplemented it's understrength regular army by raising a volunteer force for Korean service. "K-Force" volunteers were required to have had prior military service. Thus, the 'Diggers' deployed to Korea had a wealth and variety of experience. One interesting example was Private A. Croll, who'd earned the Distinguished Flying Cross and Distinguished Flying Medal in the Air Force during World War Two.

Volunteers enlisted for K-Force were given service numbers in the 400000 series. Number blocks 210000 - 212499 and 310000 - 3124999 were allocated to Australian volunteers enlisted in Great Britian. Block 340053 to 340062 was allocated to medical officers enlisted overseas. The R.A.A.F. aircrew block was 400001 - 459999. Soldiers who reentered the army after a break in service received new numbers. Thus some soldiers have as many as four numbers in their records.

Australian Army authorities provide data on medal recipients to those who can demonstrate family relationship. Medal collectors can obtain a summary sheet of the recipient's service with written permission of the recipient or his family; or if there is a record of the recipient's death or if proof of death is provided. The collector must actually possess the medals being researched.

HONORS AND AWARDS

TO ARMY

UNIT AWARDS

PRESIDENTIAL UNIT CITATIONS - 3d Bn, Royal Australian Regiment
from Republic of Korea for Kapyong-Ni, April 1951.
and the United States. See appendix for copy of U.S. citation.

INDIVIDUAL AWARDS

GEORGE CROSS - 1	PTE H.W. MADDEN[1]
C.B.E. - 2	BRIG. T.J. DALY D.S.O., O.B.E.
	BRIG. J.G. WILTON D.S.O., O.B.E.
DISTINGUISHED SERVICE ORDER - 6	LTC M. AUSTIN
	LTC I.B. FERGUSON M.C.
	LTC F.G. HASSETT M.V.O., O.B.E.
	LTC R.L. HUGHES
	MAJ J. GERKE
	MAJ A.S. MANN
O.B.E. - 17	
M.B.E. - 28	
MILITARY CROSS - 26	BAR - 1
DISTINGUISHED CONDUCT MEDAL - 4	BAR - 1 SGT W.J. ROWLINSON, R.A.R.[2]
GEORGE MEDAL - 1	NX135280 SGT T.M. MURRAY
MILITARY MEDAL - 44	BAR - 1
ASSOCIATE, ROYAL RED CROSS - 3	
BRITISH EMPIRE MEDAL - 21	
MENTION IN DISPATCHES - 107	2d M.I.D. - 2

FROM R.O.K.

D.M.S.M. TAEGUK - 1   LT-GEN ROBERTSON K.B.E., D.S.O.

Medal for Educational
and Cultural Services - 1   LT J.M. PRENTICE

FROM U.S.A.

LEGION OF MERIT - 7
DISTINGUISHED FLYING CROSS - 3
SILVER STAR - 5
BRONZE STAR w/ "V" - 1
BRONZE STAR - 5
AIR MEDAL - 3

AWARDS TO 1st Bn, ROYAL AUSTRALIAN REGT.

D.S.O. - 2   O.B.E. - 2

M.B.E. - 3   B.E.M. - 1

M.M. - 7   M.I.D. - 22

(These awards are included in the "Army" totals.)

N.A.C. #PA183677

Digger receiving an award from an American general. Original photo is uncaptioned.

(1) Private Madden's George Cross award was for prisoner of war service, as were both British awards.

(2) Sergeant Rowlinson received the only awards of the Distinguished Conduct Medal <u>and</u> Bar for Korea to British or Commonwealth forces.

AWARDS TO ROYAL AUSTRALIAN AIR FORCE

TO UNIT

PRESIDENTIAL UNIT CITATIONS - No 77 Fighter Squadron, R.A.A.F. from Republic of Korea and the United States.

INDIVIDUAL AWARDS

DISTINGUISHED SERVICE ORDER - 3   SLDR J.W. HUBBLE
                                            WC J.R. KINNINMONT
                                            WC R.T. SUSSANS

O.B.E. - 3   SLDR C.J. LEOPOLD
                     WC D.A.S. MORGAN
                     SLDR E.W. TONKIN

M.B.E. - 11

DISTINGUISHED FLYING CROSS - 47   BAR - 6

AIR FORCE CROSS - 13   BAR - 1

DISTINGUISHED FLYING MEDAL - 18   (Including 3 EIIR coinage)

AIR FORCE MEDAL - 1

BRITISH EMPIRE MEDAL - 4

MENTION IN DISPATCHES - 149

ASSOCIATE, ROYAL RED CROSS - 1

COMMENDATION FOR MERITORIOUS SERVICE IN THE AIR - 15

AWARDS TO R.A.A.F. FROM U.S.A. [1]

LEGION OF MERIT - 3

DISTINGUISHED FLYING CROSS - 19

BRONZE STAR - 1

AIR MEDAL - 113

---

(1)   U.S. awards to the R.A.A.F. listed here do not include the awards to Royal Air Force officers attached to the R.A.A.F..

AWARDS TO ROYAL AUSTRALIAN NAVY

(Including Air Squadrons)

C.B.E. - 1	CPT D.H. HARRIES
DISTINGUISHED SERVICE ORDER - 2	CPT G.G.O. GATACRE
	CPT O.H. BECHER
O.B.E. - 3	
M.B.E. - 3	LTCDR R.J. TUNSTALL
	ENG.OFF. J.B. CARTER
DISTINGUISHED SERVICE CROSS - 11	1st BAR - 2 2d BAR - 1
DISTINGUISHED SERVICE MEDAL - 3	
BRITISH EMPIRE MEDAL - 4	
MENTION IN DISPATCHES - 36	

FROM U.S.A.

LEGION OF MERIT - 8

BRONZE STAR w/ "V" - 1

AIR MEDAL - 117

ROW 1: WAR VOLUNTEER MEDAL, Reverse.
OVERSEAS OPERATIONS MEDAL, Obverse, Reverse.

ROW 2: Bars to War Volunteer Medal.

ROW 3: CROIX DE GUERRE M39-45.   James W. Lang

BELGIUM

Belgium sent one battalion of infantry which became one of the most highly respected of the allied formations. One rifle platoon was provided by Luxembourg and served as an integral part of this battalion. The Belgian (or BELUX) Battalion fought at the Imjin River battle of April, 1951 under British command and was later attached to the U.S. 3d Infantry Division. The battalion was on operations from December 18, 1950 until July 27, 1953. Two contingents served, the first being replaced in early 1952. Members were volunteers from throughout the Belgian Army. The honors and traditions of the BELUX Battalion are maintained today by the 3d Bn., Para-Commando Regiment who wear the same cap badge.

The OVERSEAS OPERATIONS MEDAL/MEDAL COMMEMORATIVE DES THEATRES D'OPERATIONS EXERIEURES was created by royal order on September 26, 1951 (M.B. du 13 OCT 51) to be a general service medal for overseas expeditions. Although only 3,587 men were eligible for this medal, including the Luxembourgers, it is a common medal as many were struck by several manufacturers.

The obverse shows the Belgian Army seal while the reverse shows the seal of the U.N.. The reverse is marked "J.DEMART 51" on the lower right. The medal uses a ring suspension.

There were two variations. The obverse coat of arms was 24mm across on the newer issue and was much smaller on the earlier issue. The signature on the earlier type was much larger.

Full size battle bars and devices were worn on the medal ribbon and the miniatures were for the ribbon bar.

BARS:	COREE - KOREA		All recipients.
	IMJIN		APR 51, 1st Contingent.
	HAKTANG-NI		APR 51, 1st Contingent.
	CHATKOL		APR 53, 2d Contingent.
WOUND BADGE:	✚		Wearer was wounded in action. Red enamel.
INDIVIDUAL CITATION:	🦁		A bronze Belgian Lion for each citation not meriting the Croix de Guerre.
INVALID RETURNED TO ACTIVE SERVICE:	☆		A silver star. Invalided and returned to active service after war wounds or service induced illness. This star had different meanings on other medals.

16

The Overseas Operations Medal was first awarded October 1, 1951 in Amsterdam when the first 450 volunteers returned from Korea. The first Belgian and Dutch soldiers to return came back on the same troopship. When the Belgian Ministry of Defense learned that the Dutch government intended to present their returnees with campaign medals upon disembarking, it hurriedly ordered this medal. Newly designed ribbon couldn't be manufactured in time so the ribbon of the Medal of the National Order of Veterans (L'Oeuvre National des Anciens Combattants) was used. Two white lines were embroidered down the ribbon (matching the U.N. colors of white and blue) instantly creating an appropriate ribbon. Both groups were then welcomed home with equal ceremony. Subsequent issues of this medal had the white stripes woven into the ribbon design.

WAR VOLUNTEER MEDAL / MEDAILLE DE VOLONTAIRE DE GUERRE

Created by Royal Order on April 7, 1952 (M.B. du 27 APR 52) for Belgian citizens and foreigners who volunteered to serve with the Belgian forces on operations ordered by the U.N. Security Council. This medal was awarded for Korea and retroactively authorized for both world wars. A further order of December 2, 1953 (M.B. du 13 DEC 53) established three bars to distinguish service in Korea or the world wars. These brass bars are worn on the ribbon and read "1914 - 1918"; "1940 - 1945" or "COREE - KOREA". Another Royal Order of November 16, 1953 established a blank bronze bar (border only, no inscription) to signify expeditionary service. To recognize actual combat service a combattants' bar was authorized. This bronze bar reads "PUGNATOR" and was not bordered. Unofficial silver bars could be purchased. This medal is not to be confused with the 1940 - 1945 Volunteers Medal of 1946.

The War Volunteer Medal is bronze. The obverse shows a shirtless warrior bearing a sword, superimposed over a large letter "V". It is marked "J. DEMART" on the reverse with "VOLONTARIIS" in large letters superior to the Belgian lion.

NOTE: The 1954 CROIX DE GUERRE has been cited in reference to Korea. As of 1968, that type had never been awarded. Korea awardees received the M39-45 issue.

LtCol Albert Crahay was decorated with the American Distinguished Service Cross for the Imjin River battle of 23 - 25 April, 1951.

LUXEMBOURG

3,587 served in the BELUX Battalion. Of these, 89 were Luxembourgers who comprised the 1st Platoon of A Company. These soldiers received the Belgian medals and awards. Luxembourg introduced a campaign service ribbon per Grand Ducal decree of May 24, 1951. This ribbon is for 'recognition to persons who distinguish themselves in time of war'. The ribbon is red-white-red with the number of blue stripes centered on the white section indicating the number of campaigns served in. One blue stripe is worn for each war or campaign service credited to the individual. This ribbon with one blue stripe would be appropriate for Korea.

The Citation of the Commandant of the Luxembourg Army was awarded to Sergeant Robert Mores.

Belgian Army Historical Section

Major Vivario, second commander of the BELUX Battalion being decorated by U.N. Commander, General Van Fleet.

ROW 1: <u>KOREA MEDAL</u>, Type III, Obverse.   <u>MEMORIAL CROSS</u>, EIIR coinage, obverse.
<u>KOREA MEDAL</u>, All types, reverse.   <u>KOREA SERVICE PIN</u>

ROW 2: Mounted 'Korea pair' with French coinage U.N. Korea Medal.
United States <u>PRESIDENTIAL UNIT CITATION</u>. From top: embroidered on olive for battledress; embroidered on forest green for post 1968 Forces dress uniform; U.S. style for P.P.C.L.I. mess dress; bullion embroidered on blue felt.

CANADA

Canada awarded the Type III KOREA MEDAL (see United Kingdom). The inscription on the Canadian Queen's Korea Medal read "ELIZABETH II DEI GRATIA REGINA" with "CANADA" appearing below the bust. Canadian issues are silver. Naming is impressed capitals with service number and name only. Award criteria were the same as for other Commonwealth participants. Approximately 27,500 Type III Korea Medals were issued.

Although the Korea Medal was instituted in July 1951, actual award of the Canadian coinage was delayed until 1954. This was the first British medal whose design was to be altered by Canada. The resultant dispute between the British and Canadian authorities was responsible for the delay.

Both the English and French language U.N. Korea Medals were officially issued. Issue was the English unless the recipient requested the French coinage, as most Francophones did. The U.N. Korea Medals were named as per the Queen's Korea. 25,584 U.N. Korea Medals in both languages were awarded to Canadians as of 1983.

The letter prefix to the Canadian service number indicated where the service-member enlisted.

A - London, Ontario
B - Toronto, Ontario
C - Ontario Province
D - Montreal, Quebec
E - Quebec City & Province
F - Nova Scotia & Prince Edward Island
G - New Brunswick
H - Manitoba Province

K - British Columbia
L - Saskatchewan
M - Alberta
N - Newfoundland (after 1948)
U - United Kingdom
P - Any other foreign land. Anyone enlisted prior to World War Two.
X - Far East

S - N.C.O.   Z - Officer   (S & Z preceded the above letter, IE: "ZE 10296".)

Soldier's service numbers that run in the 800,000 range are those individuals who joined for service in the Canadian Army Special Force, as the battalions raised for Korea in 1950 were designated. All others were regulars. Canada did not conscript during this period.

The Korea Medals to the Royal Canadian Navy are named differently from those to the Army. R.C.N. issues have only the recipient's name and number followed by either "H" or "E". The letter denoted the sailor's homeport; "H" was eastcoast, (Halifax) and "E" was Pacific coast (Esquamalt).

Unlike British issues, Canadian replacement medals are not marked as such. Medals procured from the U.K. will be marked but those struck in Canada are not. The entire Korea group in which only some of the medals are marked "Duplicate" is probably a replacement issue. Procedures for seeking replacement issues by veterans are found in CFAO 18-3. Even though the regulation provides only for replacement of medals lost through circumstances beyond the recipient's control, some abuse occurs. One recipient has replaced (and probably sold) his 'Korea pair' a dozen times, according to official records.

The style of naming can indicate the period in which the medal was issued. The very first Canadian Korea Medals were hurriedly procured and issued to the Canadian contingent to Queen Elizabeth's coronation in 1953. These and most of the 1953 and 1954 awards are named in impressed capitals. The numbers and letters are widely spaced and sometimes are slightly out of line. Most of these recipients were Special Force enlistees who were discharged after their eighteen month obligation (800 block serial numbers). Those who re-enlisted into the active force without a break in service had a 'S' prefix added to their number, IE:"SA 800267".

The majority of awards were made from 1955 - 1960. These medals are named in heavy machine engraved capitals. The numbers are properly spaced and are in line.

Awards since 1961 are either late applications for original issues or are replacement issues. Naming is in lightly machine engraved capitals. Spacing is compressed and the letters are smaller. The lettering on the U.N. Korea Medals is extremely small. Lettering on recent (1970s - 1980s) issues sometimes touch.

Naming was done under private contract to the Department of National Defense.

Only two thousand miniatures were made of the Canadian Korea Medal. They were struck by J.R. Gaunt of Montreal, Quebec and were never restruck. Most veterans used the U.K. coinages and many were unaware of a Canadian issue miniature.

R22eR Museum #SF8284

SGT Walter Zaluski, 2d Bn., Royal 22e Regiment, from Cowansville, Quebec receives the clasp of the Mention in Dispatches. He is being decorated by MGEN A.J.H. Cassels, Commander of 1 Commonwealth Division. The date is April 15, 1952.

KOREA VOLUNTEER SERVICE MEDAL

On June 17, 1991, the Minister of Veteran's Affairs announced the establishment of a Volunteer Service Medal for Korea. Queen Elizabeth II approved the creation of this medal by Order of Council of June 20, 1991. Veterans or next of kin can receive this medal upon application to the Ministry of Veteran's Affairs. All personnel of the Canadian Armed Forces who served in Korea during the period of June 27, 1950 to July 27, 1954 are eligible. This is the same qualifying period as that of the United Nations Korea Medal. The first 59 awards were made on Remembrance Day, November 10, 1991. Presentations were made by the Governor General of Canada in Ottawa. The recipients were a cross section of Korea veterans. Recipients included highly decorated ranking officers and the next of kin of soldiers killed in action.

Except for the Memorial Cross, current official Canadian practice is to issue original awards of medals unnamed. 15,000 K.V.S.M.s were struck. As of May, 1992, about 4,000 had been awarded.

The planchet is chrome plated. Detail relief of the design is not very distinct. The obverse differs from that of the Canadian Queen's Korea Medal only in the addition of a crown to the effigy of Queen Elizabeth II. The reverse inscription is "KOREA / VOLUNTEER / 1950-1954 / VOLUNTAIRE / COREE" in five lines. The reverse is encased in a wreath of leaves. A maple leaf is at the bottom center. The ribbon has seven stripes. They are blue/yellow/red/white/red/yellow/blue. The colors alude to the ribbon of the Korea Medal and the Canadian national colors. Attachment is by a brooch pin.

KOREA SERVICE PIN

This pin is given by the government to Canadian Korean War veterans when application is made by the veteran. It corresponds to similar pins awarded after the world wars but differs in that the Korea veterans had to wait thirtytwo years (1985) before their government realized that Korea was a 'real' war. The pins are serial numbered sequentially as issued. They have a clutchback attachment and an enamel finish. The design is a red maple leaf upon a white shield. The surround is green with gilt letters showing through which read KOREA·COREE·1950·1953. The serial number is stamped on the reverse.

KOREA VOLUNTEER SERVICE MEDAL; Obverse, Reverse.   Miniature.

KOREA SERVICE PIN

K.I.

P.P.C.L.I. Museum

A CANADIAN MEMORIAL CROSS RECIPIENT

On the right is L/CPL Edgely, 2d P.P.C.L.I.. He was killed in action in August, 1951. When his personal belongings were gathered, it was discovered that he had been knighted in Great Britian. The story of how a British Knight came to be a private soldier in the Canadian Army would probably be an interesting one.

CANADIAN MEMORIAL CROSS

After World War One, Canada instituted the Memorial Cross for award to the mothers and widows of the war dead. All those who died on active service were eligible except for those executed by order of court martial.

Three coinages exist, each bearing the cypher of King George V, King George VI or Queen Elizabeth II, respectively. Korean War dead were commemorated primarily by the EIIR coinage but the kin of early casualties received GVIR issues until stocks were expended. About 300 EIIR coinages were issued during the war years. Today, when a veteran's death is determined to be the result of old war injuries or disability, his survivors will be issued a EIIR Memorial Cross. Therefore, an EIIR issue won't automatically indicate a Korean War casualty.

If the casualty was married and his mother was still alive, each received a Memorial Cross. Therefore, there are sometimes two legitimate awards named to the same individual.

The medals are named by engraving on the reverse of the cross. This medal is relatively easy to rename so care should be taken by the collector when examining the specimen.

The small engraved silver strips sometimes seen with World War Two issues apparently did not accompany the Korean era awards.

The relatively low numbers of Canadian casualties makes this award rather scarce. 282 Canadians were killed in action, 38 died of wounds and 79 died of other causes. 1,202 were wounded in action.

The parameters defining "on active service" apparently were broad. For example, the Princess Pats who died in the train wreck enroute to their port of embarkation for Korea were eligible.

R22eR Museum #Z-7162-7

An award ceremony was held at Government House, Ottawa on January 26, 1953 for thirtyfive Canadian servicemen. Four of those decorated are shown here. From left to right are: CSM S. Sommerville (Military Medal); SGT B. Bergeron; (Military Medal); SGT J. Bourdeau (British Empire Medal) and Major W.H. Pope (Military Cross). All are from Quebec City.

AWARDS TO PRINCESS PATRICIA'S CANADIAN LIGHT INFANTRY

1st BN	2d BN		3d BN
D.S.O. - 2	1st Bar to D.S.O. - 1	LTC J.R. STONE DSO, MC	
O.B.E. - 1	M.C. - 1	CPT J.G.W. MILLS	O.B.E. - LTC MACLACHLAN
M.B.E. - 3	D.C.M. - 2		M.B.E. - 2
M.C. - 3	M.M. - 4		M.C. - 2
D.C.M. - 2	M.I.D. - 5		M.M. - 3
M.M. - 4	'FOREIGN' - 1		M.I.D. - 7
B.E.M. - 2			BELGIUM - 1
M.I.D. - 19			
'FOREIGN' - 4			

These awards are included in the totals in the 'Army' section on the facing page.

HONORS AND AWARDS TO CANADIANS

TO CANADIAN ARMY

COMPANION, ORDER OF THE BATH - 1	BRIG ROCKINGHAM C.B.E., D.S.O.
C.B.E. - 3	
DISTINGUISHED SERVICE ORDER - 8	2d BAR - 1 LTC STONE D.S.O., M.C.
OFFICER, O.B.E. - 17	
MEMBER, O.B.E. - 58	
ROYAL RED CROSS - 1	CPT(Matron) E.B. PENCE
MILITARY CROSS - 33	(8 GVIR coinage, 25 EIIR coinage)
DISTINGUISHED FLYING CROSS - 1	CPT P.J.A. TESS
ASSOCIATE, ROYAL RED CROSS - 1	LT(N/S) J.I. MACDONALD
DISTINGUISHED CONDUCT MEDAL - 7	1st BAR - 1 CPL MAJOR, R 22^e R. [1]
GEORGE MEDAL - 1	LCPL S.L. SINNOTT
MILITARY MEDAL - 53	(29 GVIR coinage, 24 EIIR coinage)
BRITISH EMPIRE MEDAL - 21	(4 GVIR coinage, 17 EIIR coinage)
MENTION IN DISPATCHES - 246	

FROM U.S.A.

OFFICER, LEGION OF MERIT - 4
LEGIONNAIRE, LEGION OF MERIT - 2
BRONZE STAR w/"V" - 1
BRONZE STAR - 5
DISTINGUISHED FLYING CROSS - 4
AIR MEDAL - 5

FROM BELGIUM

Officier de L'Ordre de Léopold II with Palm and the Croix de Guerre 1940 with Palm - 3	MAJ J.C. STEWART, 81 Fld Regt, R.C.A. MAJ J.E.Y. THERIAULT M.C., ", R.C.A. CPT M.H. MARCHESSAULT C.D. 3d P.P.C.L.I.
Chevalier de L'Ordre de Léopold II with Palm and the Croix de Guerre 1940 with Palm - 1	LT J. GAGNE, 3 R22eR
Chevalier de L'Ordre de La Couronne with Palm and Croix de Guerre 1940 with Palm - 1	LT R.W. BULL
Décoration Militaire 2d Class with Palm and the Croix de Guerre 1940 with Palm - 1	CPL R. PORTELANCE, 3 R22eR

(1) Corporal Major's Bar to the Distinguished Conduct Medal was one of only two Bars awarded for Korea, however, his original D.C.M. was for earlier service.

AWARDS TO ROYAL CANADIAN NAVY

DISTINGUISHED SERVICE ORDER - 1   CPT J.V. BROCK   D.S.O., D.S.C., C.D.
O.B.E. - 3
DISTINGUISHED SERVICE CROSS - 9   1st BAR - 1
DISTINGUISHED SERVICE MEDAL - 2
BRITISH EMPIRE MEDAL - 4   (2 GVIR coinage, 2 EIIR coinage)
MENTION IN DISPATCHES - 33

FROM U.S.A.

COMMANDER, LEGION OF MERIT - 1
OFFICER, LEGION OF MERIT - 4
LEGIONNAIRE, LEGION OF MERIT - 2
DISTINGUISHED FLYING CROSS - 1   LT J.J. MACBRIEN* He was the only RCN pilot to fly in Korea. He flew 66 missions from the U.S.S. Oriskany in F9F fighters.
BRONZE STAR - 1

AWARDS TO ROYAL CANADIAN AIR FORCE

O.B.E. - 1   M.B.E. - 1
DISTINGUISHED FLYING CROSS - 1   F/L GLOVER
AIR FORCE CROSS - 4
AIR FORCE MEDAL - 2   F/SGT A.A. DRACKLEY   1952
CPL G.R. REED   1953
BRITISH EMPIRE MEDAL - 2   F/SGT A.L. ENGELBERT   (both received
CPL J.B. TRUDEL   EIIR coinage)
QUEEN'S COMMENDATION FOR VALUABLE SERVICES IN THE AIR - 12

FROM U.S.A.

DISTINGUISHED FLYING CROSS - 7
BRONZE STAR - 1   S/LDR J.T. REED
AIR MEDAL - 15

22 R.C.A.F. Saberjet pilots served on postings to American fighter squadrons to gain combat experience on the F-86. They obviously did well. 426 Squadron, R.C.A.F. provided strategic airlift between North America and the Far East. Both Air Force Medals and both of the British Empire Medal awards were made in connection with this airlift.

AWARDS TO: Y.M.C.A.:   M.B.E. - 1   MISS N.E. STRONACH

SALVATION ARMY: M.B.E. - 1   J.C. SEMMENS

N.A.C. #74-11424 via Don Tresham

F/L J.A.O. LEVESQUE, R.C.A.F., scored the first Canadian aerial victory of the Korean War and Canada's first jet air to air kill on March 30, 1951. Here he is decorated with the American Distinguished Flying Cross. He also received the U.S. Air Medal for Korea and the British D.F.C. for World War Two.

R22eR Museum #SF8284

S/SGT Charles A. Stewart, 3 Bn., R22eR, receives the British Empire Medal from Major General West on October 3, 1953. S/SGT Stewart is from Quebec City.

FROM: DND/PR #PN 74-56. Press release of April 9, 1956.

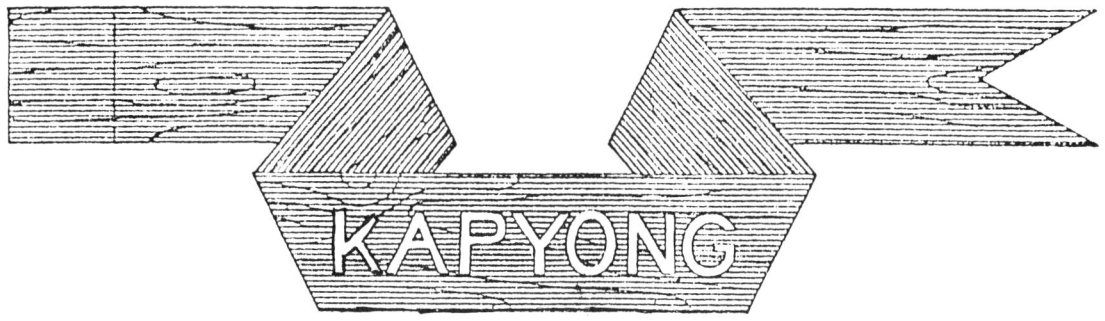

PRESIDENTIAL CITATION STREAMER

2nd Battalion,
Princess Patricia's Canadian Light Infantry

DESCRIPTION

A ribbon with a loop for the pike at one end and a swallowtail at the other end; centred on the streamer the word "KAPYONG".

DIMENSIONS

```
Total Length ------------- 38 inches
Width -------------------- 2 3/4 inches
Size of Sleeve ----------- 2 1/4 inches
Depth of Swallowtail ----- 2 1/2 inches
Height of Lettering ------ 1 1/4 inches
```

MATERIALS

The streamer is of dark sky blue watered silk, the lettering in white silk embroidery.

METHOD OF DISPLAYING

The streamer is attached to the Regimental Colour pike between the Royal Crest and the top of the Colour.

AWARDED:	PRESENTATION:
President Truman of the United States of America	Officially presented by The Honourable Douglas Stuart US Ambassador
Date: June 1951	Date: 9 June 1956

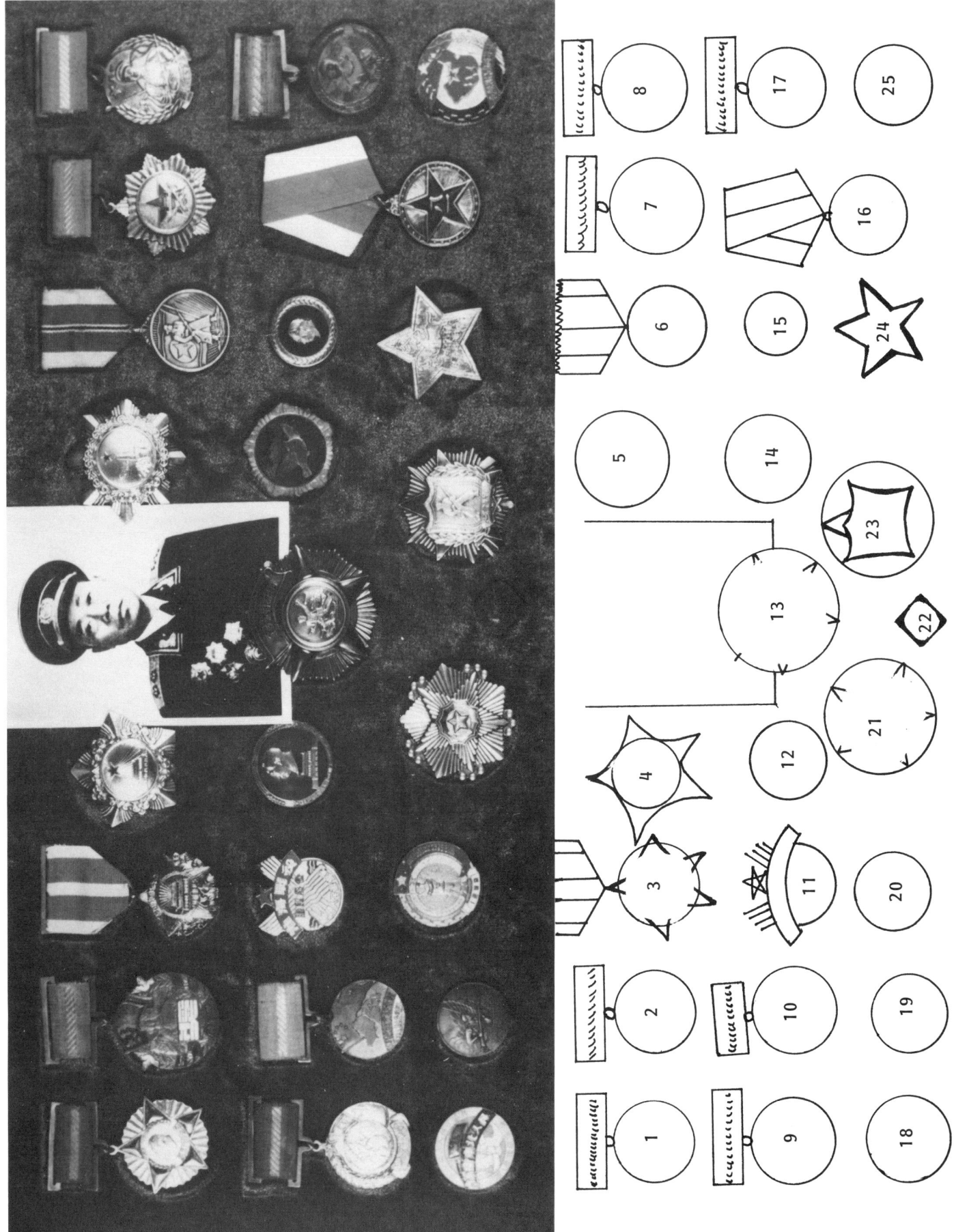

Sotheby's / David Erskine-Hill

33

CHINA
PEOPLE'S REPUBLIC OF

China had probably not intended to involve itself directly in Kim Il Sung's adventure, having it's own offensive intentions towards the Kou-Mintang government on Formosa. The advance of western armies towards China's industrial region near the Korean border caused Mao's regime to reconsider it's plans. After warnings that non-Korean troops would not be tolerated near the border went unheeded, the Chinese armies attacked. Before the Chinese offensives finally faltered in January 1951, they had inflicted the worse reverses ever suffered by American arms. From December 1950 onwards, Chinese soldiers bore the major combat burden for the communists and the Chinese high command directed the war effort.

The photograph of the awards to LTG Zhang appears courtesy of Mr David Erskine of Sotheby's of London. Most of the awards for Korea known to have been made by the Chinese were awarded to LTG Zhang. General Zhang received a wide variety of Chinese and North Korean awards and decorations, many of which are seldom seen. *Only those relevant to the Korean War are further described below. Medals are listed from left to right, top row to bottom.

1. P.R.C.: COMMEMORATIVE MEDAL FOR OPPOSING AMERICA IN ASSISTING KOREA, 1951*
2. P.R.C., SUNGJIANG PROVINCE: MEDAL FOR THE WAR TO RESIST AMERICAN AGGRES- AND AID KOREA*
3. P.R.C.: NATIONAL DAY MEDAL   1 October, 1949. for Chinese Civil War.
4. P.R.C.: ORDER OF LIBERATION   for Chinese Civil War.
5. P.R.C.: ORDER OF INDEPENDENCE AND FREEDOM   for Chinese Civil War.
6. D.P.R.C. (North Korea): MILITARY MERIT MEDAL* a frequent award to Chinese.
7. P.R.C.: MILITARY MERIT MEDAL   probably only for Chinese Civil War.
8. P.R.C.: MEDAL FOR LIBERATION OF NORTH CHINA   (Begin second row:)
9. P.R.C., LIAOHSI PROVINCE: MEDAL FOR STRUGGLE TO RESIST THE U.S. AND SUPPORT KOREA*
10. P.R.C.: MEDAL FOR LIBERATION OF NORTHWEST CHINA
11. P.R.C.: VICTORY MEDAL OF WEIHEI SEA BATTLE a battle of the Civil War.
12. P.R.C.: COMMEMORATIVE MEDAL FOR THE LIBERATION OF TIBET
13. D.P.R.C.: ORDER OF FREEDOM AND INDEPENDENCE*   see North Korea.
14. P.R.C.: VICTORY MEDAL
15. P.R.C.: COMMEMORATIVE MEDAL FOR WAR TO RESIST U.S. AGGRESSION AND AID KOREA, 1951*

16. P.R.C.: <u>MEDAL OF AUGUST 1st</u>   The planchett is hanging into the third row.
                                          For Chinese Civil War, merit in 1935 - 1937.
17. P.R.C.: <u>MILITARY MEDAL TO YUNNAN FRONTIER ARMED FORCES</u>
Begin third row:
18. P.R.C.: <u>MEDAL FOR THE DEFENSE OF THE PEOPLE OF NORTHEAST CHINA</u>
            For 1947 campaign of Chinese Civil War.
19. P.R.C.: <u>VICTORY MEDAL FOR THE CROSSING OF THE YANGTZE RIVER</u>
            For the final campaign of the Chinese Civil War.
20. P.R.C.: <u>LIBERATION OF CENTRAL AND SOUTH CHINA</u>
21. D.P.R.C.: <u>ORDER OF THE BANNER/NATIONAL FLAG</u>*   See North Korea.
22. P.R.C.: <u>COMMEMORATIVE BADGE FOR THE VICTORY AND PEACE OF THE KOREAN WAR</u>*
23. D.P.R.C.: <u>ORDER OF SOLDIER'S HONOR</u>*   See North Korea.
24. P.R.C.: <u>TENTH ANNIVERSARY MEDAL OF THE RED ARMY</u>   (1927 - 1937)
25. P.R.C.: <u>LIBERATION OF SOUTHWEST CHINA MEDAL</u>   For Chinese Civil War.

Because many of the medals for the Civil War were frequently the property of Chinese soldiers and as such, have found their way into Korean War collections, all of General Zhang's medals were identified here.

*Descriptions of the Korean War medals follows:

1. <u>COMMEMORATIVE MEDAL FOR OPPOSING AMERICA IN ASSISTING KOREA, 1951</u>

Effectively, this is the Chinese campaign medal for Korea. As the Chinese communist government wasn't officialy "in" Korea, this medal was presented to the "volunteers" by the People's Political Consultive Conference National Committee.

The medal is gilt brass with the points of the star in red enamel. The horizontal gold stripe on the red ribbon is embroidered in diagonal bands. Attachment is by a simple wire safety pin. This ribbon, suspension and attachment is common to many P.R.C. medals. Most are cheap in appearance.

The obverse characters translate as "Oppose America, Aid Korea, Commemorative". The reverse inscription credits the above committee for the award.

2. <u>MEDAL FOR THE WAR TO RESIST AMERICAN AGGRESSION AND AID KOREA ; SUNGJIANG</u>

This medal was awarded to the Chinese People's Volunteers by Sungjiang Province which has a large Korean ethnic population. The medal is enamel on brass and the ribbon and attachment is as #1.

The obverse inscription is (approximately) "Medal honoring the vanguards in resisting the U.S. and supporting Korea, 1951". The reverse reads: "Issued for the people of Sungjiang Province".

9. MEDAL FOR THE STRUGGLE TO RESIST THE U.S. AND SUPPORT KOREA; LIAOHSI

This medal is from Liaohsi Province to the Chinese People's Volunteers. Most of the C.P.V. passed theough Liaohsi Province enroute to Korea. Liaohsi was absorbed by Liaoning Province in 1954. This region also has a scattered Korean population.

The ribbon, suspension and attachment is the same as on the P.R.C. Commemorative Medal. The planchett is crudely cast bronze. On the obverse, below the star, is a map of Korea. The North Korean and Chinese flags are on the right, the Korean flag superior. The inscription translates as "Medal to commemorate the struggle to resist the U.S. and support Korea". The reverse reads "The people of Liaohsi Province", "Peking Great Medal Factory".

14. VICTORY MEDAL or PEACE MEDAL

This badge was issued by the Chinese forces to C.P.V. officers to commemorate the end of the war. It was issued on October 25, 1953. It is made of gilt brass and red enamel. The obverse characters read "Glorious Peace". The reverse inscription translates as "War to resist U.S. aggression and aid Korea". This was struck in two sizes.

15. COMMEMORATIVE MEDAL FOR WAR TO RESIST U.S. AGGRESSION AND AID KOREA

This was presented to C.P.V. senior officers in March, 1951, during the first visit of the Central Contingent. It is made of gilt brass and red enamel.

22. COMMEMORATIVE BADGE FOR THE VICTORY AND PEACE OF THE KOREAN WAR

This badge was issued to all Chinese People's Volunteers and to North Korean officials on September 18, 1952, on the occasion of the second visit of the Central contingent. This small bronze badge shows a Picasso dove surmounting the date "1952". The attachment is a wire safety pin. The reverse is plain.

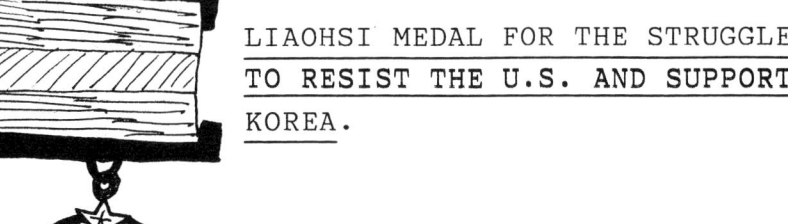

9.

LIAOHSI MEDAL FOR THE STRUGGLE TO RESIST THE U.S. AND SUPPORT KOREA.

Reverse inscription:

奎壬旨大另赔
(stamped serial number)

北京大勛拔丙製
(the underlined characters are unclear in the sample seen)

ROW 1: <u>COMMEMORATIVE MEDAL FOR OPPOSING AMERICA IN ASSISTING KOREA, 1951</u> Obverse, Reverse. <u>COMMEMORATIVE MEDAL FOR THE ANTI U.S. WAR IN KOREA ISSUED BY THE CHINESE RAILROAD DEPARTMENT</u> Obverse, Reverse.

ROW 2: <u>1953 PEACE MEDAL</u> Obverse, Reverse. <u>SINO - SOVIET FRIENDSHIP MEDAL</u>

COMMEMORATIVE MEDAL FOR THE ANTI U.S. WAR IN KOREA ISSUED BY THE CHINESE RAILROAD DEPARTMENT

This cumbersome title is also the translation of the obverse inscription. The ribbon, attachment and suspension are identical to the P.R.C. Commemorative Medal. The planchet is brass with an enamel face. A white peace dove surmounts a steam locomotive approaching from between full color North Korean and Chinese flags. The background is medium blue. The brass inscription shows from a white background.

SINO - SOVIET FRIENDSHIP MEDAL

This soviet style medal was awarded in connection with the Sino - Soviet industrial cooperation of the 1950s. It is possible that it was awarded to Soviet officers associated with the Chinese Peoples Volunteers, perhaps the cadre responsible for training the MIG-15 crews. This is a Chinese award made to Soviet citizens, but a direct link to the Korean War has not been confirmed.

The medal is red enamel on brass. The red ribbon is folded about a metal plate to give it the soviet style five sides. The two yellow stripes can vary in width considerably. The reverse is marked with the year, examples noted read "1951", "1952", and "1953". The title on the lower obverse reads: 中蘇友誼萬歲.

There are probably other provincial or central government awards for Korea. Numbers of Chinese awards have begun to come onto the market, but unfortunately, background data concerning these medals does not seem to be accompanying them.

ROW 1: <u>KOREA CAMPAIGN MEDAL</u>; Obverse, Reverse.

ROW 2: <u>COLOMBIAN INFANTRY BATTALION MEDAL</u>, Type 2; Obverse, Reverse.

COLOMBIA

Korea was Colombia's only foreign war, not including U.N. peacekeeping duty. Colombia sent one infantry battalion (through four rotations) and a frigate. The battalion arrived on June 15, 1951 and was attached to the U.S. 31st Infantry, 7th Division. 4,314 soldiers and about 1,000 sailors served.

KOREA CAMPAIGN MEDAL   This is a bronze medal with the seal of the Republic of Colombia on the obverse with the Spanish inscription "REPUBLICA DE COLOMBIA/ FUERZAS MILITARES" (Republic of Colombia/Military Forces). The reverse shows the taeguk with the inscription "CAMPAÑA DE COREA" (Korean Campaign). This style of open brooch is common to all the medals described here.

COLOMBIAN INFANTRY BATTALION MEDAL, KOREA 1953   Colombia's heaviest losses of the war were suffered on March 23-24, 1953 on the 'Old Baldy' position. The mountain was lost when the Chinese attacked while the Colombians were relieving their forward positions. This was the beginning of a series of hill battles which was to culminate the next summer on the adjoining Pork Chop Hill.

This battle was commemorated by award of the Colombian Infantry Battalion medal, struck on the order of LTC Ruiz-Novoa. A small number, probably no more than fifty, were struck in Japan. These are silver, with a wreath added to the bottom third of the planchet. The medal is 30mm across. The obverse shows a soldier holding the Colombian flag atop a mountain. The flag is enamelled yellow/red/blue, from top to bottom. The reverse shows the rampant lion sleeve insignia of the Colombian Battalion. Above this is the inscription "BATTALION DE INFANTERIA COLOMBIA - CAMPAÑA DE COREA", below are the dates "1952 - 1953". On a raised tablet are the words "HONOR/AL DEBER COMPLIDO" (Honor to those who fulfill their duty). The ribbon is coarsely woven. Vertical stripes are blended together in a rainbow effect with red into yellow, then green and blue. The pinback brooch has "COREA" on a solid back and frame.

The more common later version has the rectangular open brooch common to the Colombian medals. "CAMPAÑA DE COREA" and the dates were deleted from the reverse. The ribbon has seven vertical solid stripes. From the left is red/ orange/yellow/light green/dark green/blue/purple. Perhaps this second type wasn't a later version but the enlisted men's medal. The original fifty made up by the battalion commander may have just been for his officers.

A version with a bronze planchet exists also. Recently (1991), bronze medals have appeared for sale that supposedly are made from original surplus production found at the factory. Details on the planchet differ from earlier examples. They have the first type ribbon and the second type (open) brooch.

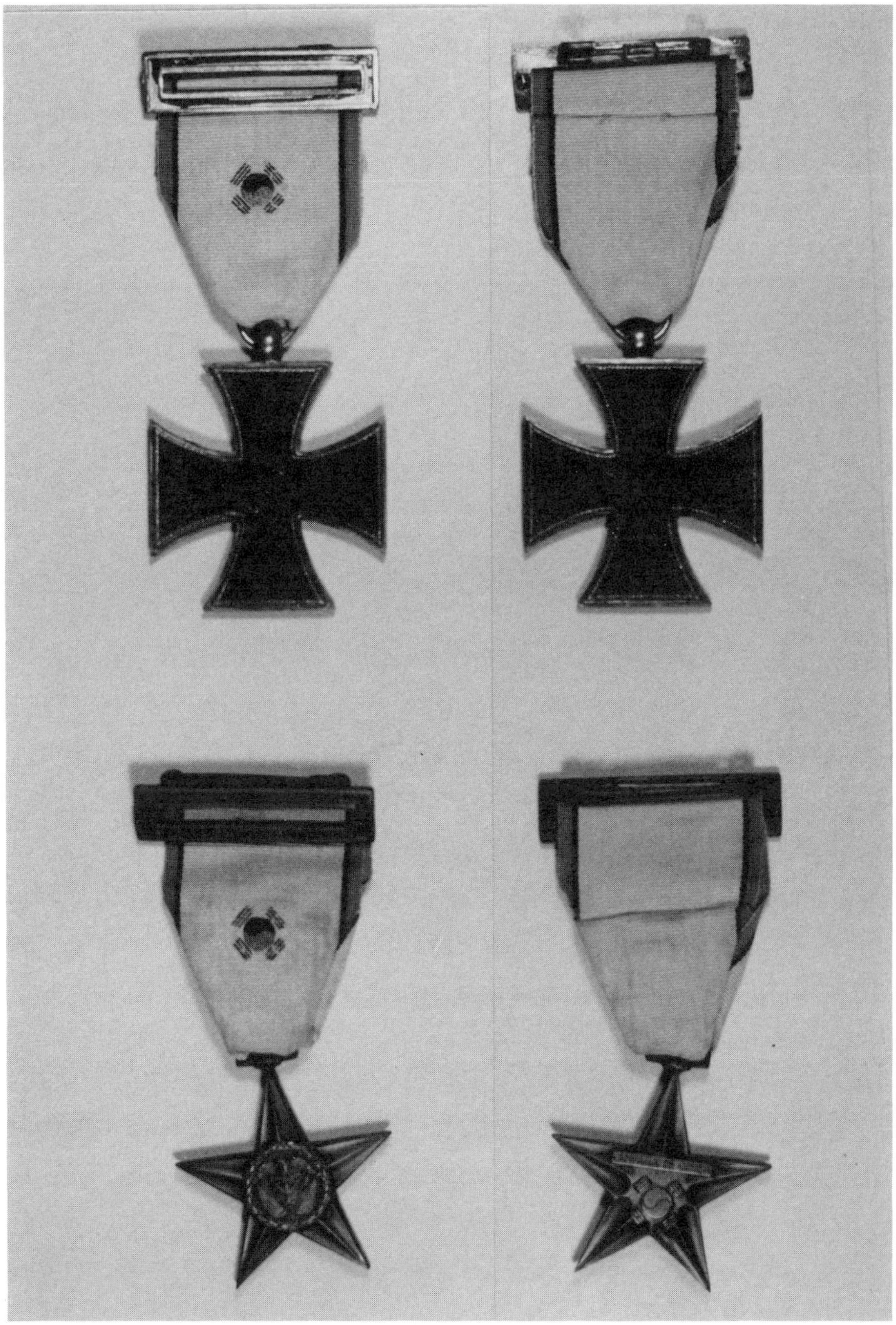

ROW 1: <u>IRON CROSS / CRUZ DE HIERRO</u>; Obverse, Reverse.
ROW 2: <u>VALOR STAR / ESTRELLA DE VALOR</u>; Obverse, Reverse.

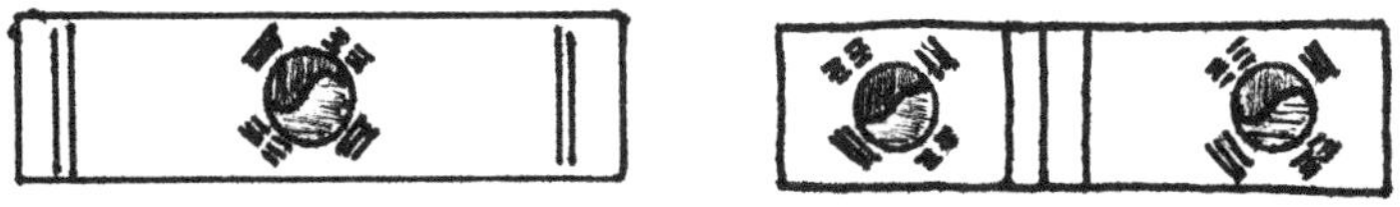

ESTRELLA DE VALOR   CRUZ DE HIERRO

<u>RIBBON BARS</u>

41

VALOR MEDALS

These medals, and the wound badge, were established by President Arbelaez through Decree 0812 on March 27, 1952. Both medals use the same open frame pin back brooches and ribbon. The ribbon has the R.O.K. taeguk symbol centered on a white ribbon. The ribbon is bordered by the Colombian national colors of red/blue/yellow from inside to outside. These medals aren't named nor numbered. They could be awarded posthumously. Together, they comprise the series "La Condecoracion Servicios en Guerra Internacional".

IRON CROSS / CRUZ DE HIERRO   The inspiration for this medal appears obvious. It is silver with black enamel finish. On the obverse center is the Colombian national seal. The reverse, in common with the other medals, has the taeguk in the center. On the left branch of the cross (on the reverse) is the inscription "ACCION/DISTINGUIDA/DE VALOR" in three lines. "CAMPAÑA/DE/COREA" is on the right branch in three lines.

The ribbon bar is enameled silver and is attached with two knurled nuts. The design has the Colombian national colors slightly off center with a taeguk at each end of the bar.

VALOR STAR / ESTRELLA DE VALOR   This bronze medal resembles the American Bronze Star but is larger. The center obverse is the Colombian national seal. On the reverse center is the inscription "CAMPAÑA DE COREA" on a raised bar superior to a taeguk.

This medal also exists as a miniature. The ribbon bar has the same design as the ribbon with the taeguk centered. Construction of the ribbon bar is the same as that of the Cruz de Hierro.

BADGE FOR WOUNDED IN COMBAT / DISTINCTIVO HERRIDOS EN COMBATE   This badge is 45mm x 15mm. The frame is gilt and the background is red enamel. A blue enamel type is for the air force. One 3/16th inch bronze star is added per wound. Attachment is by knurled nut or as with more recently manufactured examples, clutchback. The earlier knurled nut issues had a faint black border around the red. 131 Colombians were killed and 448 were wounded. 505 badges were awarded to 12 officers, 109 N.C.O.s and 384 enlisted men.

COMBAT INFANTRY BADGE FOR INTERNATIONAL CONFLICT   The title is self descriptive. Construction is similar to the wound badge.

Perhaps one of the highest honors to the Colombian Battalion was the statement by an American general who said that the Colombians were the bravest soldiers that he'd seen in three wars.

HONORS AND AWARDS
UNIT
U.S.A. P.U.C. - 9 DEC 52 (for action 12-23 OCT 51, Kumsong)
U.S.A. P.U.C. -

COLOMBIA
HONOR AL DEBER CUMPLIDO WITH "V" - 114*
HONOR AL DEBER CUMPLIDO - 237*
IRON CROSS - 117
VALOR STAR - 4,314

R.O.K.
ULCHI D.M.S.M. - 1   LTC RUIZ-NOVOA

U.S.A.
LEGION OF MERIT - 2
SILVER STAR - 18
BRONZE STAR WITH "V" - 25   LTC RUIZ-NOVOA
BRONZE STAR - 9

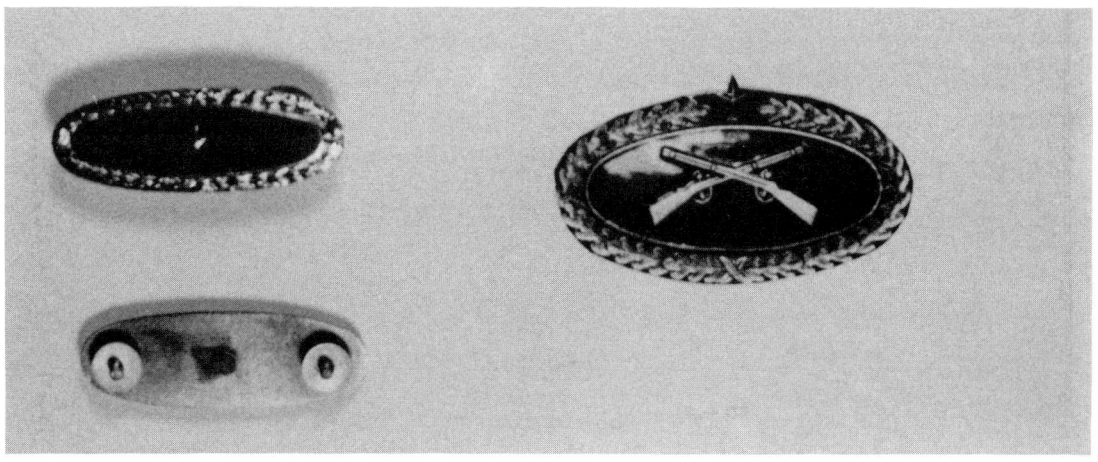

WOUND BADGE; Top - Obverse, Bottom - Reverse.
COMBAT INFANTRY BADGE FOR INTERNATIONAL CONFLICT   James W. Lang

*The official R.O.K. history uses these descriptions. They are probably the "Old Baldy" medals.

R.O.K. Embassy (U.S.A.)

Col. Polania (U.S. Bronze Star), Lt B. Lema-Henao and 1st Cpl Espinal-Mejia (U.S. Silver Star) with their Battalion colors after being decorated.

James W. Lang

<u>JUTLANDIA MEDAL</u> Obverse, Reverse

DENMARK

Danish awards are a challenge due to the low number awarded and the requirement that they be returned on the death of the recipient.

JUTLANDIA COMMEMORATIVE MEDAL KOREA 1951 -53 / ERINDRINGSMEDALLION FOR DELTAGELSE I HOSPITALSKIBET JUTLANDIA EKSPEDITION TIL KOREA 1951 - 53.

The Jutlandia was a hospital ship manned by the Danish Red Cross. This ship served three tours of five to eight months each. Personnel were rotated each trip. About twentyfive percent of the hospital staff was female.

The Jutlandia Medal was founded by King Frederik IX on January 17, 1956. Manufacture was by the Royal Danish Mint in Copenhagen. 480 were awarded. This medal has been faked.

The medal is silver, 31mm in diameter. The obverse shows the bust of King Frederik IX. The inscription reads "FREDERICUS IX REX DANIAE". The reverse is surrounded by an oak wreath, 'JUTLANDIA' was inscribed above the ends of the wreath with "KOREA / 1951 - 1953" in the center in two lines. These were neither numbered nor named. The ribbon has two broad white vertical stripes on red.

DANISH RED CROSS PRISONER OF WAR EXCHANGE MEDAL / KRIGFANGE UDVEKSLING MEDALJE

This medal was founded on September 2, 1956 by the Danish Red Cross. The 1914 - 1919 issue of the Red Cross Medal was used to make these. This medal is easy to fake as the details from the 1914 - 1919 medal can be erased and the Korean era engraving substituted. This is especially dangerous to collectors as this was how the originals were prepared. Only nine Danish doctors served on the exchanges so the originals are obviously extremely rare. These are neither numbered nor named.

The P.O.W. Exchange Medal is silver with a red enamel cross on the obverse. The cross on the reverse was engraved "KOREA / KRIGSFANG / UDVEKSLING / 1953". The medal was awarded with a U.N. certificate dated September 8, 1953. These certificates, and presumably, the medals were awarded to these nine doctors: V. Asschenfeldt-Hansen; H. Boland; A. Christiansen; T. Christiansen; H. Jacobsen; S. Jensen-Hein; P. Kirketerp; B. Maegaard-Neilson; and H. Vinter.

ETHIOPIA KOREA MEDAL; Obverse, Reverse.

ETHIOPIA

The Ethiopian Army sent one infantry battalion which was drawn from the Imperial Guard. The 1st Kagnew ("Conquerors") Battalion arrived in Korea on May 7, 1951. The 2d Kagnew Battalion arrived on March 29, 1952 and was relieved by the 3d Kagnew Battalion on April 16, 1953. The 4th Kagnew Battalion arrived after the cease fire. 3,518 combat personnel served with the first three battalions. The Ethiopian battalions never lost an inch of ground nor was a single Ethiopian soldier captured by the enemy. The Ethiopian Red Cross sent a cadre of nurses to treat Ethiopian wounded recovering in the hospitals in Japan.

The Ethiopian KOREA MEDAL is one of the handsomest of the Korean War series. This medal came in a large 'court' size (52 x 63mm) and a regular issue which is 35 x 45mm. Both types apparently use the same size ribbon. The medal is made of silvered white metal. The obverse consists of the Imperial Crown surmounting a trefoil. The portrait of Emperor Haile Selassie is centered. Inscribed in Amharic on the reverse is "We support every nation's independence but we are always the enemies of aggression / Korea / 1943" (per Ethiopian calendar).

HONORS AND AWARDS
ETHIOPIA

KNIGHT OF THE ORDER OF EMPEROR MANELIK 1 - LTC IRGETU, Teshome
"highest gallantry award" - 2LT MAMO, Haptewold[1]

R.O.K.

PRESIDENTIAL UNIT CITATION - Platoon of 3 Co., 3d Bn. for Outposts Yoke and Uncle, May 19, 1953.

ULCHI D.M.S.M. - 4	COL GUEBRE, Kebbede
	LTC ANDARGUE, Asfaw
	LTC SHITTA, Wolde Yohannis
	LTC IRGETU, Teshome
WHARANG w/ SILVER STAR - 1	2LT GETAHUN, Aseffa
WHARANG D.M.S.M. - 2	2LT MAMO, Wolde H.
	2LT ASFAW, Zeneke[2]

---

1. The R.O.K. War History stated that 2Lt Mamo won Ethiopia's "highest gallantry award". I was unable to determine what that was during this period.
2. It was 2Lt Zenebe's platoon that won the R.O.K. Presidential Unit Citation.

Ethiopia (con't)

AWARDS FROM U.S.A.

PRESIDENTIAL UNIT CITATION - 2d KAGNEW BATTALION
For Hills 602 and 700, near Samhyon, September 16 - 26, 1952.
Awarded October 15, 1952.

LEGION OF MERIT - 2	LTC IRGETU, Teshome
	LTC ANDARGUE, Asfaw
SILVER STAR - 1	CPT WALDETENSYE, Tefera
BRONZE STAR - 18	CPT WALDETENSYE, Tefera
	CPT WANDEMU, Negatu
	CPT WORKNEW, Sium
	CPT GIZAW, Merid
	CPT ASSEFA, Mesheshe
	CPT TESEMMA, Tammat
	1LT GEMEDA, Desta
	1LT BERHANU, Tariku
	1LT WOLDS, Tesfay
	2LT KASSAHUN, Abeba
	2LT GEBRESUS, Mickael
	SGT KEBEDE, Molla
	PVT GIFAR, Fitalla
	PVT TESSEMA, Negga
	PVT ISHETA, Hailemarial
	PVT WOLDE, Kasaye
	PVT KENATE, Bayesa
	PVT MESHESHA, Haile

Those who are interested in learning more about the achievements of these remarkable soldiers should refer to "Pork Chop Hill" by S.L.A. Marshall. Many of the Bronze Star actions are recounted in Volume One of the R.O.K. "History of the U.N. Forces".

U.N. #40418

Private Gabremicail Tumebo, who lost his leg in Korea, was another of a number of decorated Korean War veterans to be invited to the U.N. Headquarters on May 25, 1953.

ROW 1: <u>KOREA CAMPAIGN MEDAL</u>; Variation with ring suspension.   John J. Barnes
       Standard coinage, Obverse, Reverse.
ROW 2: <u>CROIX DE GUERRE T.O.E.</u> with Palm; Obverse, Reverse.
       <u>VOLUNTEER COMBATTANT CROSS</u> with Bar KOREA; Obverse.

FRANCE

The Battalion Francaise - Organisation des Nations Unies (BF-ONU) was another all-volunteer expeditionary group. The French Battalion had an enviable combat record and a slightly piratical air about it. Members came from all branches of the French Army, including the Foreign Legion. Many were World War Two veterans who returned from civilian life. The BF-ONU suffered very heavy casualties in Korea but met its ultimate fate in another war. The 'Battalion Coree', consisting mostly of Korea veterans, was wiped out by the Viet-Minh in one of the final, tragic battles of the First Indochina War.

3,763 served with the BF-ONU; of these, 280 were killed, 1,008 wounded, 12 were prisoners and 7 missing.

MEDAILLE COMMEMORATIVE FRAINCAISE des OPERATIONS de O.N.U. en COREE

The French Korean Campaign Medal was established by the Defense Ministry on 8 JAN 52. Two months service in Korea or on fleet operations offshore was required. Service ended by wounds also qualified. Recipients of the Croix de Guerre also qualified without regard to period of service.

The design is by Robert Louis and the medals were made by Delannoy.

Foreigners who were attached to the BF-ONU for two months, and who were so allowed by their own government, could also receive this medal.

The planchet is bronze and 36mm across. The Korean Taeguk is superimposed over freedom's torch, the design surrounded by the olive branches from the U.N. seal. The bar suspender is in the shape of a pagoda's roof. The planchet attaches to the bar with a ring. There are two varieties of suspension. The most common has the ribbon pass behind the bar for its full width. A variation uses a ring above the bar through which the ribbon passes in the American style. The example shown also had an American made safety pin style attachment.

The rim of the reverse reads "REPUBLIQUE FRANCAISE". In much smaller horozontal print, the inscription reads "MEDAILLE COMMÉMORATIVE FRANCAISE des OPERATIONS de l'ORGANISATION des UNIES EN COREE".

The colors of the ribbon represent the colors of the U.N. and the national colors of France.

CROIX DE GUERRE des THEATRES d'OPERATIONS EXTERIEURES

This valor award was created on April 30, 1921 to honor deeds performed while on 'expeditionary operations' during France's many colonial wars. An order of January 23, 1957 included Korea as an eligible campaign. The Croix de Guerre des T.O.E. is similar to those of the world wars but differs in the reverse inscription. The red/white/red ribbon is suspended from a brass rod. Multiple awards are indicated by the addition of palms onto the ribbon. Five bronze palms are replaced by one silver palm.

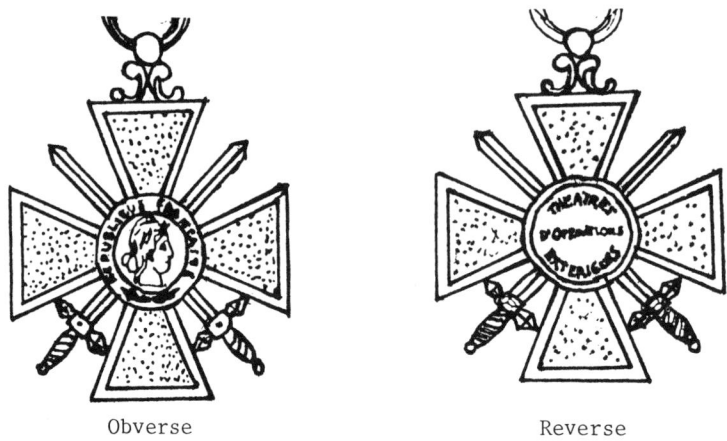
Obverse   Reverse

The CROIX DU COMBATTANT VOLONTAIRE / COMBAT VOLUNTEER'S CROSS is awarded to those who volunteered for combat service. This medal has remained essentially unchanged from the First World War. The obverse is the left facing head of a Great War soldier. The medal was bronze. More recent issues are gilt "stay-bright". The colors of the ribbon are taken from those of the three military decorations: the Croix de Guerre, the Medaille Militaires and the Legion d' Honneur.

On September 8, 1980, a bar was instituted for Korea. The white metal, slip on bar reads "COREE" and is framed.

Obverse

ECPA #52 114 09

In August, 1952, Captain Sendre was decorated with the Croix de Guerre T.O.E. and the American Bronze Star Medal. He is also wearing the ribbons of the U.N. Korea Medal and the French Korean Campaign Medal. Above the ribbons is an American Combat Infantry Badge. On his left shoulder is the lanyard of the Medaille Militaire awarded the Battalion.

French lieutenant receiving a decoration from officers of the U.S. 23d Infantry.

AWARDS TO BF-ONU

UNIT AWARDS

FRANCE

L'ORDRE DE L'ARMEE – 4 AWARDS   (EQUAL TO CROIX DE GUERRE T.O.E. with PALM)

      1: Ministry of National Defense Orders No 6, 27 FEB 51
         (for Chipyong-Ni)

      2: M.N.D. Orders No 26,   4 JUL 51

      3: M.N.D. Orders No 39, 26 OCT 51

      4: M.N.D. Orders No 16, 11 APR 53

FOURRAGERE de MEDAILLE MILITAIR des T.O.E.; M.N.D. Orders No 39, 10 NOV 53

KOREA

PRESIDENTIAL UNIT CITATION – 1   20 NOV 52   (for multiple actions)

U.S.A.

PRESIDENTIAL UNIT CITATION – 3 Awards

      1: 8 Army General Orders 86, 20 FEB 51
         (for period 30 JAN – 2 FEB 51; Chipyong-Ni)

      2: 8 Army G.O. 49, 11 JUL 51
         (for period 13 – 15 FEB 51; Hongchon)

      3: Dept. of Defense G.O. 72, 9 AUG 52
         (for period 16 –22 MAY 51)

In addition, the Battalion Pioneer Platoon received two awards of the L'ORDRE de L'ARMEE for actions in which the platoon was annihilated.

Collective unit awards were worn on the unit colors.

AWARDS TO BF-ONU

TO INDIVIDUALS

FRANCE

CROIX de LEGION d'HONNEUR; COMMANDER - 1

CROIX de LEGION d'HONNEUR; OFFICIER - 7

CROIX de LEGION d'HONNEUR; CHEVALIER - 2

MEDAILLE MILITAIRE - 193

CROIX DE GUERRE des T.O.E. - 2,898

KOREA

WAR SERVICE MEDAL - All members of BF-ONU per R.O.K. M.O.D. General Orders 282, 3 DEC 53.

ULCHI D.M.S.M. - 1	LTC De GERMINY, Francois	38943
CHUNGMU with GOLD STAR - 2	MAJ DeTURBET, Marcel	000903
	MAJ ALEXANDRE, Robert	
CHUNGMU with SILVER STAR - 2	CPT de BAZELAIRE de LESSEUX, Joseph	422
	1LT DUROUCHET, Jaques	753
CHUNGMU - 3	1LT REYNAUD, Gabriel	1947
	1LT BASTIDE, Gilbert	194
	1LT PERRON, Francois	
WHARANG with GOLD STAR - 1	2LT LECARD, Jean Louis	2081
WHARANG with SILVER STAR - 2	2LT FEUVAL, Vincent	289
WHARANG - 1	SFC CAPRON, Marcel	3144

All awards per R.O.K. M.O.D. General Orders 358, 21 SEP 53.

On October 8, 1953, the French Battalion awarded a number of medals to it's Korean augmentees. Details were not available.

U.S.A.

DISTINGUISHED SERVICE CROSS - 1   SGT MISSERI, Louis

SILVER STAR - 30   LTC BORREIL, Francois
MAJ DeSAGE, Bertrand
CPT COUPIL, Robert   (1953)
1LT FLEURIEU, Jacque D.
1LT LIRON, Jean P.
2LT LECARD, Jean
1LT PERRON, Francois
1LT ROGER, Jean
SGT MISSERI, Louis (also D.S.C.)

BRONZE STAR - 8

COMBAT INFANTRY BADGE - 1

LEGION OF MERIT - 1   LTC deGERMINY, Francois   (1953)

ECPA #CTT 18623

Three soldiers of the BF-ONU wear their newly awarded American Silver Stars.

UNITED NATIONS KOREA MEDAL - GREEK; Obverse, Reverse.
DISTINGUISHED CONDUCT MEDAL

GREECE

Greece deployed one infantry battalion (through several rotations) and a C-47 equipped air transport flight. 10,581 Greeks served from December 9, 1950 until December 11, 1955. 1,286 became casualties.

Greece did not award it's own campaign medal but there was a Greek language striking of the U.N. Korea Medal. The R.O.K. government awarded the Greeks the R.O.K. War Service Medal. The Greek Battalion was the most heavily decorated infantry battalion in the war, according to an American statement to a U.N. session on December 8, 1953.

HONORS AND AWARDS
AWARDS TO UNIT
GREECE

COMMANDER, CROSS OF VALOR

WAR CROSS, 1st CLASS

R.O.K.

P.U.C. - GREEK EXPEDITIONARY FORCE BATTALION

P.U.C. - FLT.13, Royal Hellenic Air Force (Hagaru-ri, DEC 50)

U.S.A.

P.U.C. - Greek Bn.; 8 Army G.O.16, 7 JAN 52 (Soneyok 3-10 OCT 51)

P.U.C. - Greek Infantry Co.-Korea 11 DEC 55

P.U.C. - FLT.13, R.H.A.F. (For service, 1 DEC 50 - 31 MAR 53)

D.U.C. - 3 Co., Greek Bn.; 16 NOV 54 (Hill 420, Iron Triangle, 17-18 JAN 53)

INDIVIDUAL AWARDS
GREECE

ROYAL ORDER OF GEORGE 1st - 1

GRAND COMMANDERS ORDER OF THE PHEONIX WITH SWORDS - 2

GOLD CROSS OF VALOR - 121   PVT PIROYAKIS, Dimitrios

SILVER CROSS OF VALOR - 186

WAR CROSS, 2D CLASS - 13

WAR CROSS, 3D CLASS - 760

DISTINGUISHED CONDUCT MEDAL - 2,069

FLYING CROSS OF VALOR - ?

BATTLEFIELD PROMOTIONS - 27

R.O.K.

ULCHI D.M.S.M. - 5

CHUNGMU D.M.S.M. - 45

WHARANG D.M.S.M. - 9

WAR SERVICE MEDAL - 9,410

U.S.A.

(Awards to September 30, 1954)

LEGION OF MERIT - 7   LTC KOUMANAKOS, Georgios

SILVER STAR - 46

BRONZE STAR WITH 'V' - 122

BRONZE STAR - 223

BELGIUM

CROIX d'OFFICIER de L'ORDRE DE LA COURONNE AVEC PALME - 6

COLOMBIA

MEDAL 'HONOR AL DEBER CUMPLIDO' OF THE COLOMBIAN ORDER - 1*

NOTES: The first award of the Gold Cross of Valor in Korea was to Private Drankopoulas Stayos. He was the first Greek soldier killed in action in Korea.

LT SPYRIDON, Alevizakos (LTC, retd):   GOLD CROSS for VALOR; WAR CROSS;
U.S.A. valor award;
R.O.K. and U.N. War Service Medals;
battlefield promotion.

* This is probably the "Old Baldy" medal. The Greek Battalion had also fought over that position.

U.N. via George Forty

MG William Hodge, Commander of IX Corps, presenting a decoration to Colonel I. Daskalopoulos, Commander of the Greek Battalion. April, 1951.

ROW 1: <u>VIDESH SEVA</u> Obverse, Reverse.

ROW 2: <u>GENERAL SERVICE MEDAL, 1947</u> BAR "OVERSEAS KOREA 1950-53".

G.S.M. courtesy James W. Lang.

INDIA

India's role in Korea was unique. Even then, India was establishing her preeminence among emerging nations who wished to be "non aligned" in the East-West struggle. As such, Indian diplomats were unofficial contacts between the Red Chinese and th U.N. members. Even with a small military unit engaged as part of the U.N. forces, India's credentials as a neutral were sufficient for both sides to accept Indian supervision of the P.O.W. screening and participation in the Neutral Nations Repatriation Commission.

India awarded two medals for service in Korea. The soldiers received one or the other and sometimes both.

Indian medal groups from this period often contain British awards as medals earned with the Viceroy's Indian Army were authorized to be worn after independence. Long service Indian groups often contain other U.N. service medals as India has continued to be a leading supporter of U.N. peacekeeping operations.

GENERAL SERVICE MEDAL 1947 BAR "OVERSEAS KOREA/1950-53"

This medal is awarded for service in specified campaigns. At least seven bars have been issued to date including "OVERSEAS KOREA/1950-53". Personnel must have seen operational service in Korea between December 20, 1950 and July 27, 1953. Time spent as a prisoner of war counted in the required period of service (the length of which I was unable to determine). Service terminated by disability, wounds or death also qualifies.

This medal is 35mm in diameter and is made of cupro-nickel. The obverse is the 'Divine Sword', the reverse is a lotus flower with buds. The red silk ribbon hangs from a straight bar suspender.

OVERSEAS MEDAL/VIDESH SEVA/ Clasp कोरिया

"KOREA' (in Hindi) was one of at least seven clasps/bars awarded this medal. The Videsh Seva is awarded to servicemembers for foreign service, except those on diplomatic duty. The length of service required to earn this medal varied with the length of the tour of duty. If the tour was less than one year, three months service qualified. For tours of one year or more, six months was required. Service terminated by disability, wounds or death qualified. Award is automatic if a gallantry medal is earned. The Korea bar service period is November 22, 1950 to March 17, 1954.

The Videsh Seva is cupro-nickel and 35mm in diameter. The obverse is an ancient warship and the reverse is a "swelling sea". Superior to the sea is the Hindi script for 'Videsh Seva': विदेश सेवा मैडल . The cobalt blue ribbon is divided by five thin, white vertical lines.

GALLANTRY AWARDS

<u>MAHA VIR CHAKRA</u> "Conspicious acts of gallantry in the presence of the enemy"... This is India's second highest gallantry award.

<u>VIR CHAKRA</u> "Acts of gallantry in the presence of the enemy"... This is India's third ranking gallantry award.

<u>MENTION IN DISPATCHES</u> The Indian M.I.D. is a miniature lotus leaf on the ribbon of the campaign medal and ribbon bar.

An article detailing Indian awards and decorations can be found in "The Medal Collector" Vol.22 No.8, Aug 77.

HONORS AND AWARDS

INDIA

MAHA VIR CHAKRA - 2	LTC RANGARAJ (O.C. 60 PARA FLD AMB)
	MAJ BANERJEE, N.B. #MR-281
VIR CHAKRA 1st BAR - 1	MAJ RANGASWAMI, V.P.
VIR CHAKRA - 6	CPT DAS, N.C.
	CPT BANERJEE, A. #MR-381
	NAIK SINGH, Ratan
	NAIK SINGH, Nagsen
	NAIK SINGH, Umrao
	L/NAIK SINGH, Budh
2d M.I.D. - 1	CPT BANERJEE, A. #MR-381
MENTION IN DISPATCHES - 25	

KOREA

CHUNGMU D.M.S.M. - 4

U.S.A.

U.S. ARMY MERITORIOUS UNIT CITATION - 1   60 (PARACHUTE) FIELD AMBULANCE
BRONZE STAR - 2

As India had no rotation policy, original members of 60 Field Ambulance served through all three winters in Korea. Except for the Koreans, this was unique amongst the United Nations forces.

NEUTRAL NATIONS REPATRIATION COMMISSION

To supervise the P.O.W. exchanges, India sent out, as part of the N.N.R.C., the 190th Infantry Brigade with four battalions. These were: 5 Rajputna Rifles; 6th Jat; 3d Dogra and 3d Garwal Rifles, with supporting services. 60 (Para) Field Ambulance was taken under command for the duration. 190 Brigade was soon joined by 2d Bn., Indian Parachute Regiment. Indian troops were eligible for the same awards for Korean service as part of the N.N.R.C. as when they were under U.N. command, except for the U.N. Korea Medal. The N.N.R.C. was disbanded in March, 1954.

Other member states were Switzerland, Poland and Czechoslovakia. The Swiss apparently did not award anything in connection with N.N.R.C. service. It has not been determined if anything was awarded to the Poles and Czechoslovakians.

OBVERSE   REVERSE

Ribbon with Merit Award

Ribbon with War Service Device

ITALIAN RED CROSS MEDAL FOR SERVICE IN WAR ZONE

ITALY

The Italian Red Cross Hospital No.68 with 128 personnel served in Korea. Those eligible members received an Italian striking of the United Nations Korea Medal, of which 131 are said to have been awarded. It appears that most Italian recipients obtained and wore the english coinage. This is probably due to the late (1964) authorization of the italian coinage by the Italian government.

In this case, the U.N. Korea Medal was awarded to citizens of a nation that wasn't a member state, Italy not joining until 1955. The Italian Hospital deployed at the request of the International Red Cross in Geneva. The U.N. medal was authorized for members of national chapters of the Red Cross but not for personnel of the International Red Cross. The U.N. Command General Orders No.18, 22 July, 1952, certified the Italian Red Cross Hospital as having directly supported U.N. military operations. This established the eligibility of members for award of the U.N. medal according to U.N. award criteria.

The 128 members of Hospital 68 included 19 officers, 8 nurses, 12 non-commissioned officers and 89 other ranks. The hospital commander, Major Fabio Pennacchi, received the Korean Chungmu D.M.S.M. with Gold Star on orders dated August 18, 1954. Members received an Italian Red Cross service medal.

Hospital 68 received two awards of the Korean Presidential Unit Citation dated October 6, 1952 and December 20, 1954.

ITALIAN RED CROSS MEDAL FOR SERVICE IN WAR ZONE

This medal exists in gold, silver and bronze classes. The same ribbon is used for all three classes. The ribbon is white and is bordered by the Italian national colors of red/white/green. The red is outermost at each end.

War zone service is indicated by a bronze palm centered on the ribbon and ribbon bar. A star centered on the palm is a merit award. The ribbon devices will be of the same metal as the medal itself.

Medals without the palm are for territorial service only.

ROW 1: MILITARY MERIT MEDAL: Obverse, Reverse.
FATHERLAND LIBERATION COMMEMORATION MEDAL:[1] Obverse, Reverse.
ROW 2: FREEDOM AND INDEPENDENCE ORDER:[2] Obverse, Reverse.
ROW 3: ORDER OF THE NATIONAL FLAG, 3d Class: Obverse, Reverse.
NORTH KOREA - CHINA FRIENDSHIP BADGE

(1) Dave Cabral, Joe Shields, Orders & Medals Society of America. (2) James W. Lang

DEMOCRATIC PEOPLE'S REPUBLIC OF CHOSUN
NORTH KOREA

The North Korean People's Army and Air Force shocked the Republic of Korea and it's American advisors with a surprize blitzkreig which very nearly succeeded. Only a combination of an overextended offensive with a last moment rally of the U.N. army saved the Republic of Korea. The Chinese intervention which saved the D.P.R.C. at it's last moment allowed the N.K.P.A. to achieve a remarkable recovery. Although the Chinese effectively led the communist effort after 1950, the N.K.P.A. remained an extraordinarily tough, disciplined and effective force whose ruthlessness was second to none.

Although North Korea issues a wide variety of orders, decorations and medals, only those pertinent to the 1950 - 1953 war are covered here. Many of these awards are still presented, although mostly in modified form. They could be awarded to individuals, groups or organizations. Several are authorized for foreigners.

TITLE OF HERO OF THE CHOSUN D.P.R. / GOLD STAR MEDAL   This Title is the D.P.R.C.'s highest award. The Gold Star Medal is only part of the award, which really is a title. This was established on June 30, 1950 to honor 'heroic exploits in war'. A recipient of this title will also receive the Order of the National Flag, First Class and a Scroll of Honor from the Supreme People's Assembly. A statue of the recipient is erected at his birthplace.

TITLE OF LABOR HERO OF THE CHOSUN D.P.R.   This title is seperate from the above but is considered to be of equal status. It was established on July 17, 1951. The recipient receives all of the above honors and awards plus a gilt hammer and sickle badge. The title is conferred on those who perform great feats in industry, farms or any labor oriented job which contributed greatly to the war effort.

ORDER OF THE NATIONAL FLAG / KUKKI HUN CHANG   Established on October 2, 1948, this medal was awarded for outstanding valor or service above and beyond the call of duty. It can be awarded for military deeds or political, cultural or economic achievements as well.

This decoration was awarded in 1st, 2d and 3d Class levels which are made of gold, gold and silver and silver, respectively. The reverse inscription translates as "Chosun National Flag Order (1st)(2d)(3d) Class". Early issues were serial numbered.

FREEDOM AND INDEPENDENCE ORDER   This medal is a combat award and was presented in two classes. 1st Class was to division and brigade commanders and 2d Class was to commanders at other levels. Award was to commanders who "display bravery" and whose victory made an outstanding contribution to the war effort. The reverse inscription reads 자유·독립훈장 .

SOLDIERS HONOR MEDAL   This decoration is for acts of individual heroism in combat. It was awarded to ranks up to second lieutenant. This is also in two classes which are gold (1st) and silver (2d). The points of the star are in red enamel. The lettering on the scroll is 조국을위하여. The reverse inscription is 전사의영예훈장 / 제二급 / 제 호   (3 lines)

ORDER OF LABOR / NOYOK HUN CHANG   This award is still made and was almost certainly presented for wartime achievement. It was established on July 17, 1951. It was awarded to those who distinguish themselves in a "revolutionary task or construction project". The massive effort of maintenance and reconstruction required to sustain the war effort under the allied air onslaught probably inspired the creation of this decoration.

MILITARY MERIT MEDAL / KUN KONG /군공메달   The KUN KONG was established on June 13, 1949. Award required ten years of service "and in recognition of their meritorious achievement in combat, counter-infiltration operations and in the fight against foreign aggression". This was also awarded to the Chinese 'volunteers'.

There are three coinages of this medal, two of which are postwar issue. Type one, the wartime issue, came with a rough textured ribbon and was usually serial numbered. The type one obverse shows a Korean soldier advancing with a soviet moisin type rifle while the second issue changed some background details and the third type updated the rifle to an AK-47.

FATHERLAND LIBERATION COMMEMORATION MEDAL / CHOKUK HEAPANG KIYOM /조국해방기념메달

The CHOKUK HEAPANG KIYUM was established on July 25, 1985 "on occasion of the fortieth anniversary of the foundation of the Korean Workers Party...and to commend those who fought with devotion during the time of righteous Fatherland Liberation War that opposed the American invaders and their tools military invasion.."

The medal is a light gilt color with a red background and red ribbon. The inscription on the reverse reads 조국해방기념 메달

DISABLED VETERANS HONOR MEDAL   This was awarded by the president of the Supreme Peoples Council to those who were disabled while in the service. Not illustrated.

K.I.

SOLDIERS HONOR MEDAL: Obverse, Reverse, screw attachment.

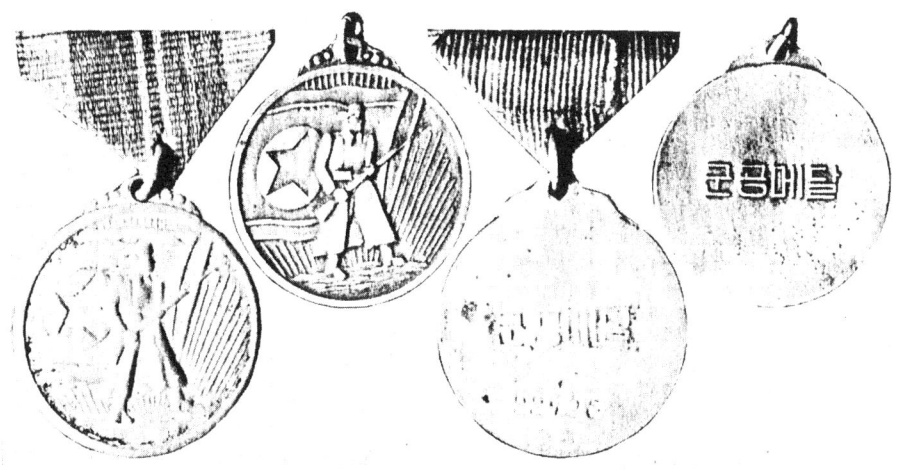

MILITARY MERIT MEDAL

WHICH ONE DO YOU HAVE? CONDUCTED BY THE EDITOR

ABOVE IS THE SO-CALLED "MILITARY MEDAL FOR MERITORIOUS SERVICES AND DISTINGUISHED DEEDS" OF NORTH KOREA. THE EXAMPLE WITH THE RIBBON IS THE GENUINE ISSUE, WHILE THE MEDAL WITHOUT RIBBON IS A COUNTERFEIT PREPARED FOR THE COLLECTOR TRADE.

THE GENUINE PIECE HAS A RATHER SOFT DESIGN, IS OF SILVER OR SILVERED METAL, IS NUMBERED ON THE REVERSE, AND HAS A ROUGH-TEXTURED RIBBON OF BLUE (EDGES & CENTER), RED (INNER FLANK), AND PINK (CENTER FLANK AND OUTER FLANK) OVER A METAL FORM WITH CRUDE PINBACK BROOCH.

THE COUNTERFEIT IS A MORE FORCEFUL EXECUTION OF THE DESIGN, BUT IS APPARENTLY A CASTING IN SOME GREYISH SOFT METAL. NOTICE THE CASTING POCK MARKS ON THE REVERSE. NONE OF THESE HAVE BEEN SEEN FITTED WITH ANY KIND OF RIBBON, JUST A RING THROUGH THE MEDAL LOOP. AS THE ORIGINAL IS SELDOM SEEN, THIS SPURIOUS FABRICATION COULD FOOL THE UNSUSPICIOUS.

Reprinted from the May, 1964 issue of "The Medal Collector" with permission of the Orders and Medals Society of America.

REPUBLIC OF KOREA - SOUTH KOREA

The Republic of Korea bore the major burden of the war and paid the highest price. The front passed over Korea several times and left the people, crops and cities devestated. The Korean veteran who lived to receive his U.N. Medal certainly didn't think that he'd fought for 'the principles of the U.N. Charter'. The Korean soldier seldom fought with the material abundance of his allies. He looked forward to no rotation or even discharge, his service ended with the receipt of a Special Wound Medal or Next of Kin Award. His draft board was frequently a military police press gang and he often went directly to the front with only a few hours training. Never the less, the 'ROKs' often fought stubbornly and well. By the cease-fire, the R.O.K. Army had developed into an effective and modern force. In addition, South Korea raised an efficient tactical air force entirely from scratch. Basic flight training was performed on actual combat missions in the early days. The story of South Korea's fight for existence deserves to be far more widely known.

The Republic of Korea developed a full range of orders, awards and decorations for government, military and civilian service and achievement. Only those most relevant to the military aspects of the 1950 - 1953 war are described here.

The R.O.K. government maintains strict controls over the medals it awards. Serial number rolls are maintained. As it is illegal for a R.O.K. citizen recipient to sell his medals, the government has been known to 'spot check' the recipients years later. The decorations are highly regarded and it is considered very disrespectful to sell them. Accordingly, most of the serial numbered medals on the market were to foreign recipients. The R.O.K. authorities are not forthcoming with assistance to researchers and collectors.

The order of precedence for period military awards is: ORDERS OF MILITARY MERIT 1st - 4th CLASS - ORDERS OF CULTURAL MERIT - MEDALS OF MERIT (DEFENSE MEDAL) - 1st CLASS SPECIAL WOUND MEDAL - 2d CLASS WOUND MEDAL - 1950 - 1953 WAR SERVICE MEDAL - FAMILY OF KILLED IN ACTION AWARD - GUERRILLA WAR SERVICE MEDAL.

Commonly used designs are based on the mugungwha flower or leaf. The mugungwha or Rose of Sharon is the national flower of Korea. The taeguk (ying-yang) symbol has its origin in the Buddist religon. It is properly worn with the red over the blue.*

A bronze mugungwha leaf on the ribbon represents multiple awards.

*The example on the cover has the ribbon mounted incorrectly,

PRESIDENTIAL UNIT CITATION

The Presidential Unit Citation was awarded in the name of the President of the Republic to South Korean and allied units which displayed great gallantry under extremely hazardous conditions.

It is authorized for permanent wear by members of American units who were assigned to the unit during the period for which the award was made. The American made version has the same metal gilt frame as the United States P.U.C., the open end of the "V" shape being worn facing up. The red of the taeguk is worn superior to the blue. The ribbon colors are the same as those of the War Service Medal except that the base color of the Unit Citation is white, rather than yellow.

U.N. KOREA SERVICE MEDAL - KOREAN

PRESIDENTIAL UNIT CITATION   Top: Korean made example. It is covered with a ¼ inch thick piece of plastic.   Bottom: U.S.A. made example.

ROW 1: <u>WAR SERVICE MEDAL</u>; Obverse, Reverse. <u>DEFENSE MEDAL</u>

ROW 2: <u>WAR SERVICE MEDAL</u>; 1st Type.   <u>WAR SERVICE MEDAL</u>; Belgian coinage. <u>GUERRILLA WARFARE SERVICE MEDAL</u>

Although official Korean publications list the first type War Service Medal and the Guerrilla War Service Medal, it is uncertain whether they were actually produced or exist in statute only.

WAR SERVICE MEDAL / JUNE 25 INCIDENT PARTICIPATION MEDAL   The second is the Korean term for the War Service Medal, as it is more commonly known. The early version is a star with a map of Korea on the central part. It was established in October, 1950. The far more common type with the round planchet was established in April, 1954. The second type retained the map of Korea and added a pair of crossed shells below the map and a laurel wreath surrounding both. The reverse has only a Korean inscription that means "KOREA - WAR SERVICE MEDAL". The ribbon can be seen with or without the taeguk. Several allied contingents received the War Service Medal. The United States was offered but rejected the blanket award to its troops.

Earlier examples had a brown finish applied while more recently manufactured examples are of a better quality bronze. This medal has been struck in South Korea and Belgium.

GUERRILLA WAR SERVICE MEDAL   This medal was awarded for service in suppressing rebellions and in the counter guerrilla campaigns of the late 1940s.

DEFENSE MEDAL   This award is from the Merit Medal series, the planchet design of which is the same throughout. The medals differ only in the ribbon and bar. This award is for meritorious service to the defense of the nation or for life-saving at the risk of one's own. The design is centered with a taeguk and features a mugungwha blossom. The ribbon is white-blue-white, the blue symbolizing justice. The bar reads 방위포장 which means "DEFENCE MEDAL".

ORDER OF MILITARY MERIT / DISTINGUISHED MILITARY SERVICE MEDAL
These decorations are made for gallantry or meritorious conduct in combat or in military service. The Order of Military Merit has four classes: Taeguk; Ulchi; Chungmu and Wharang. Each class has three grades: 1st (Gold Star); 2d (Silver Star) and 3d Grade (no star). The stars are worn on the ribbon and ribbon bar. The medals are made of enameled brass or silver. They are colorful, attractive and well made, especially in comparison with the service medals. The reverse inscription on each medal reads, in Korean: "KOREA / DISTINGUISHED SERVICE MEDAL / 1st - 4th GRADE" (as appropriate) with the serial number stamped below. Records of the recipients are maintained by the R.O.K. government and each piece is serial numbered.

(D.M.S.M.) ORDER OF MILITARY MERIT - TAEGUK   This is the highest military decoration. The sun rays of the medal represent national strength and the mugungwha with the supporting poles, solid national foundation. The ribbon is light blue with four white stripes at either side. These colors represent the purity of the Korean people.

D.M.S.M. - ULCHI   Ulchi is the family name of a great military leader of the Kokuyo dynasty. The sword, staff and baton represent military honor and discipline. The brown ribbon represents dignity. There are three white stripes at either side of the ribbon.

D.M.S.M. - CHUNGMU   Chungmu honors a great admiral of the Yi dynasty, Yi Sun Shin. The turtle shell represents the quality of the armed forces and the turtle shaped battleship honors Yi Sun Shin. The ribbon is light blue with two white stripes at each side.

D.M.S.M. - WHARANG   The Wharang were knights of the Silla dynasty who were renowned for their honor, integrity and courage. The helmet and arrows represent the martial arts; the ruby, loyalty and the mugungwha leaf symbolizes prosperity. Courage and devotion are represented by the reddish-yellow ribbon. The ribbon has one narrow white stripe near each side.

TAEGUK
1st CLASS D.M.S.M.

ULCHI
2d CLASS D.M.S.M.

ROW 1: <u>WHARANG</u> D.M.S.M.; Obverse, Reverse.
ROW 2: <u>CHUNGMU</u> D.M.S.M. w/Silver Star; Obverse, Reverse.
ROW 3: Ribbon bar; <u>CHUNGMU</u> w/ Silver Star.

ROW 1: <u>ALLIED KOREAN WAR VETERAN'S MEDAL</u>:
Lapel pin; Miniature; Full size obverse, Reverse.

ROW 2: <u>STANDARD WOUND MEDAL SECOND CLASS</u>;
<u>SPECIAL WOUND MEDAL FIRST CLASS</u>, Obverse, Reverse.

AMBASSADOR OF PEACE / ALLIED KOREAN WAR VETERANS MEDAL   This medal is sponsored by the (R.O.K.) Korean War Veterans Association. Allied veterans on K.W.V.A. sponsored tours and reunions in Korea are awarded this medal during formal ceremonies by the Koreans. This medal was first awarded in 1975. Approximately 10,000 had been awarded by 1990. A set of cuff links and a tie clip bearing the design from the lapel pin complete the set. The medal set is presented in a red velvet lined case with an award document with copies in English and Korean. Variations exist that lack the 'Korean War Veteran' bar and are not gilt finished. The set pictured is gilt brass with an enamel taeguk on the full size medal and lapel pin.

WOUND MEDALS

FIRST CLASS SPECIAL WOUND MEDAL   This badge is for those whose wounds are disabling, such as loss of sight or a limb. It is silver gilt. The taeguk is centered on a red enamel cross. The star is silver gilt and in turn is centered on five blue enamel branches.

The reverse inscription is 대한민국 특별상이기장 which translates as 'Special Wound Badge'.

SECOND CLASS WOUND MEDAL   All other war wounded receive this medal. It is suspended from a ribbon which is predominately red, bordered light blue with two narrow white stripes. The reverse inscription is 대한민국 상이기장 which means 'Wound Badge'.

FAMILY OF KILLED IN ACTION AWARD   This is a mugungwha blossom mounted on a cord. There is a similar badge for families of National Policemen killed in action.

FAMILY OF KILLED IN ACTION AWARD

R.O.K. award presentation to Filipino soldier.

U.N. #36724

Proxy award of Korean Medal of Military Merit (as described in the original caption) to Colonel Dionysio S. Ojeda, former commander of the 10th Battalion Combat Team. Maximo Bueno is shown receiving the medal on behalf of Col. Ojeda in Pusan on April 2, 1952. In the center is Captain Liberato Salvador who is wearing the ribbon of the American Korean Service Medal on his left side. He is also wearing what appears to be embroidered versions of the Philippine and U.S.A. Presidential Unit Citations.

MALAYSIA

A Malay Air Force headquarters squadron deployed to Korea during the fall of 1950 to provide ground to air communications support.

The PINGAT KHIDMAT BKRANIFORM MALAYSIA/GENERAL WAR SERVICE MEDAL was awarded to anyone who qualified for the U.N. Korea Service Medal. The English language U.N. medal was awarded.

As Malaysia didn't become independent until 1958 and the British medals were awarded during the colonial period, the award of the Malaysian G.S.M. might have been retroactive.

The reference to this is a letter from a former member of the squadron whose medals are shown here.

James W. Lang

ROW 1: <u>CROSS FOR JUSTICE AND FREEDOM</u>: 3 award bars, Obverse.
Reverse of unmounted medal & mounted.

ROW 2: Mounted group awarded to Dutch sailor.

L to R: <u>CROSS FOR ORDER AND PEACE</u> (for Indonesia War of Independence); <u>CROSS FOR JUSTICE AND FREEDOM</u>; <u>U.N. - KOREA</u>, Dutch coinage; South Korean <u>WAR SERVICE MEDAL</u>.

NETHERLANDS

The Netherlands contributed one infantry battalion and five warships in rotation. The infantry wore the brass cap badge of the Van Houten Regiment and was attached to the U.S. 38th Infantry. The battalion was manned by volunteers from throughout the Dutch army and marine corps. Korean service with the Dutch Contingent U.N. Forces - Korea (N.D.V.N.) was recognized by award of the "CROSS FOR JUSTICE AND FREEDOM / KRUIS VOOR RECHT EN VRIJHEID".

A royal decree established the Kruis Voor Recht en Vrijheid on July 23, 1951. The "J" on the center obverse stands for "Juliana" and the reverse center shows the Dutch Lion symbol. The medal itself is silvered.

A combat clasp styled like a roman sword with a laurel wreath could be earned and was worn on the ribbon. A one tour clasp read "KOREA 1950", second and third tours had the numbers "2" and "3" superimposed on the laurel branch. Multiple tour bars were added onto the ribbon and did not replace the earlier clasp.

This medal is neither numbered or named but the Chancellor of the Netherlands Orders was ordered to keep a roll of awardees. The medal could be revoked or not issued if the servicemember's conduct was bad or 'lacking in devotion'. The Cross was first presented by HRH Prince Bernard to the First Contingent upon their return from Korea. The ceremony was in Rotterdam on October 1, 1951.

Dutch military personnel are not allowed to wear foreign military insignia without specific governmental permission. A general permission was granted for the U.N. Korea Medal; the R.O.K. War Medal and the R.O.K. and American Presidential Unit Citations.

In March, 1990, the Minister of Defense, A.L. ter Beck, announced the institution of a wound badge. Eligible personnel are all (former) servicemembers wounded in action since May 9, 1940. Due to the late authorization of this award and the probable low number of potential recipients who will apply for it, this award will seldom be seen with Korean War medal groups. Approximately 645 Dutch soldiers were wounded in action in Korea.

Dutch privacy laws are very strict and do not allow the release of information concerning medal recipients unless proof of relation or death can be shown.

MEDAL OF TRIBUTE OF THE ROYAL NETHERLANDS SOCIETY "OUR ARMY" FOR THE KOREAN FIGHTERS - 1951.

This medallion was awarded by the above society and is not a government award. As such, it is not authorized on the uniform and was not made to be worn. It was probably presented on January 8, 1952. The inscription indicates that this wasn't awarded to naval personnel.

The medalion is 50mm across. It is made of frosted bronze. The design is well defined. The obverse shows the Dutch Lion superimposed over a column of marching soldiers. Across the flagstaff is the inscription ONTWAAK ('alert' or 'awake'). Overhead flies the Dutch flag. The center stripe of the flag is inscribed "NEDERLANDSCHE VEREENINGING / ONS LEGER" (Netherlands Society/Our Army). The reverse is plain with this inscription in six lines: "HULDE VAN DE/KON. NED. VER./ONS LEGER/AAN DE/KOREASTRIJDERS/1951".

Obverse   Reverse

MILITARY ORDER OF KING WILLIAM

LTC DEN OUDEN, Marinus Petrus	12 FEB 51	K.I.A.
LT ANEMAET, Johannes	14 FEB 51	
PFC KETTERING - OLIVIER, Johan	12 FEB 51	K.I.A.

Three awards were made of Holland's highest military honor. All were won during the Dutch Battalion's stand at Hoengson, February 12 - 14, 1951. Two of these awards were posthumous. For this battle, the battalion's first major engagement, it earned it's first American Presidential Unit Citation.

The Military Order of William must be returned to the government upon the recipient's death.

Photo courtesy of the Society of the Military Order of William.

S.M.G.L.

LTC MARINUS P. Den OUDEN

LTC Den Ouden was the commander of the first contingent. On February 12, 1951, a Chinese unit attacked his headquarters after posing as friendly Korean troops. He reacted swiftly, rallying his troops and was killed by a grenade in the resulting melee. LTC Den Ouden is seen here decorating his troops with the American Silver Star.

S.M.G.L. #IUB-04138

LT JOHANNES ANEMAET

Seen here as a captain after the war, Lieutenant Anemaet alone lived to wear his order. He led his platoon in a bayonet charge to repulse a Chinese attack on Hill 325, near Wonju. He retired from the Army as a major general in 1976.

S.M.G.L. #2C-1-7908

PVT JOHAN FRANS KETTING - OLIVIER

Dutch soldiers in the winter of 1951, shortly before the Hoengson - Wonju battle. Private Ketting - Olivier is on the far right. He was killed in the same fight as LTC Den Ouden.

S.M.G.L.

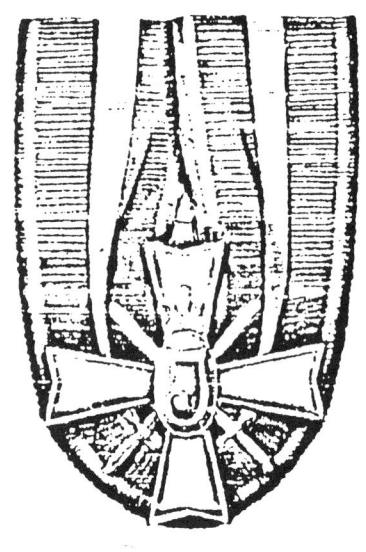

DE MINISTER VAN MARINE,

GELET OP HET KONINKLIJK BESLUIT VAN 23 JULI 1951, nr 30,

KENT TOE

HET KRUIS VOOR RECHT EN VRIJHEID

MET DE GESP
„KOREA 1950"

AAN:

matroos der 1e klasse,

H. de Jong (39362).

's-GRAVENHAGE, 25 October 1951.

DE MINISTER VOORNOEMD,

Award certificate for the Cross of Justice and Freedom.

HONORS AND AWARDS TO N.D.V.N.

UNIT AWARDS

R.O.K.

PRESIDENTIAL UNIT CITATION - "For Battalion's contribution"
R.O.K. Ministry of Defense General Orders 271, September 2, 1953.

U.S.A.

PRESIDENTIAL UNIT CITATION - 2   for Hoengson - Wonju, February 12, 1951.
                                                            for Soyang River, May 16 - 22, 1951.

INDIVIDUAL AWARDS

NETHERLANDS

MILITARY ORDER OF WILLIAM, 4TH CL - 3
BRONZE LION - 5
BRONZE CROSS - 19
CROSS OF MERIT - 4
CROSS FOR JUSTICE AND FREEDOM - 3,972   (total including with clasps)
...with clasp "2" - 516   (including two nurses)
...with clasp "3" - 38

R.O.K.

	total	officer	N.C.O.	other ranks
ULCHI D.M.S.M. - 3		3		
CHUNGMU with GOLD STAR - 6		6		
CHUNGMU with SILVER STAR - 12		12		
WHARANG with GOLD STAR - 7		7		
WHARANG with SILVER STAR - 15		4	6	5
WAR SERVICE MEDAL - all ranks				

U.S.A.

LEGION OF MERIT - 4		4		
SILVER STAR - 14	CPL GROEN, Hendrik H.			
		8	3	3
BRONZE STAR - 62		9	33	20

KOREA MEDAL MEMORIAL CROSS John Zabarylo

Not to scale.

NEW ZEALAND

The New Zealand forces were in Korea from December 31, 1950 until November, 1954. 3,794 soldiers served with 'K-Force' in Korea, most with 16 Field Regiment, New Zealand Artillery. The Navy kept two frigates on station throughout the war with six vessels serving a total of eight rotations. 1,350 sailors served off Korea.

The Korea Medal to New Zealanders differs from United Kingdom issues only in the naming. Korea Medals to soldiers were impressed with the recipient's service number, rank and name. More recent issues add the corps after the name, IE: "204724 DRIVER M.A. MEKII N.Z.A.S.C.". The 16th Field Regiment medals are indicated by "R.N.Z.A.". Most service numbers are six digit figures and give no indication of place of enlistment or service branch. Medals to sailors were unnamed or were impressed in very small capitals.

The <u>NEW ZEALAND MEMORIAL CROSS</u> is silver. The next of kin of a servicemember who was killed or died on active service were eligible. Award apparently wasn't limited to the spouse and mother. Naming is on the reverse in small impressed capitals. This is a rare award for Korea. Twentytwo soldiers and one sailor were killed in action, with sixteen other deaths. Korea awards are EIIR coinage.

HONORS AND AWARDS
R.O.K.

PRESIDENTIAL UNIT CITATION - 16 Field Regt, R.N.Z.A.

INDIVIDUAL AWARDS
BRITISH EMPIRE

ARMY		NAVY	
C.B. - 1	BRIG. R.S. PARK	D.S.C. - 5	1st Bar - 1
D.S.O. - 4			2d Bar - 1
M.B.E. - 14	(9 to 16 Fld Regt)	M.B.E. - 1	
M.C. - 10		D.S.M. - 2	
B.E.M. - 5		M.I.D. - 18	
D.C.M. - 1	GNR D.E. RIXON R.N.Z.A.		
M.M. - 7			
M.I.D. - 50	(45 to 16 Fld Regt)		
"FOREIGN" - 4	(including 1 AIR MEDAL from the U.S.A.)		

KOREA MEDAL; Obverse, Reverse.

Norway Ministry of Defense

NORWAY

Norway sent a field hospital which served in Korea from July 19, 1950 until November 10, 1954. This hospital was administered first by the Norwegian Red Cross, then from November 1, 1951, by the Norwegian Army. A total of 623 medocal and service personnel served with "NORMASH" (Norwegian Mobile Surgical Hospital). NORMASH served as an independent mobile surgical hospital. It was employed similarly to the famous U.S. Army M.A.S.H. units. Members were volunteers, primarily reservists. They served a minimum six month tour of duty which did not count against their required period of military service. NORMASH treated over 90,000 patients and was highly regarded.

Members received the Norwegian KOREA MEDAL and the english language U.N. Korea Medal.

The Korea Medal was authorized by Royal Decree on April 29, 1955. Eligibility required two months service overseas, including transit time. The Korea Medal was awarded in person by Prince Olav in Borgården at Akerhus Castle in Oslo on October 2, 1955. It may be awarded posthumously.

The Korea Medal is bronze. The obverse design is the arms of the realm. On the reverse the flags of Norway, the United Nations and South Korea are set inside laurel branches. Outside these branches are the words "NORSK · FELTSYKEHUS · 1954" (Norwegian Field Hospital Korea 1954). Below the design are the dates "1951 - 1954". The medal isn't numbered or named. The ribbon colors are taken from the flags of the Norwegian Royal Navy and Merchant Fleet. The vertical stripes are navy/white/red/white/navy.

At present, there are no orders of dress in the Norwegian Army on which medals are worn.

AWARDS TO NORWAY MOBILE SURGICAL HOSPITAL

UNIT AWARDS

R.O.K.

PRESIDENTIAL UNIT CITATION - 2 2 NOV 52; OCT 53.

U.S.A.

U.S. ARMY MERITORIOUS UNIT CITATION

NORWAY con't.

INDIVIDUAL AWARDS
R.O.K.
ULCHI D.M.S.M. w/ GOLD STAR - 3
ULCHI D.M.S.M. w/ SILVER STAR - 2

U.S.A.
OFFICER, LEGION OF MERIT - 1
LEGIONNAIRE, LEGION OF MERIT - 1
MEDAL OF FREEDOM w/ BRONZE PALM - 1
BRONZE STAR - 11

R.O.K. Embassy (U.S.A.)

The Norway - Korea Medal award ceremony at Akerhus Castle, Oslo, on October 2, 1955.

Sometimes mistaken for the Korean Medal is the NORWAY - KOREA FRIENDSHIP SOCIETY MEDAL. This medal is struck in bronze. The obverse features the Norwegian and South Korean flags in full color enamel. The surrounding lettering is "NORSK KOREAFORENING". The reverse is bordered by laurel branches and is otherwise blank.

ROW 1: <u>KOREA CAMPAIGN MEDAL</u>: Obverse, Reverse, ribbon bar and lapel pin.

ROW 2: <u>PRESIDENTIAL UNIT CITATION</u>;
<u>U.N. KOREAN SERVICE MEDAL - TAGALOG</u>: Unofficial Filipino coinage made by El Oro Company.

PHILIPPINES

The contribution of the Philippines is better appreciated when one remembers that the Philippines were fighting a communist insurgency in their own homeland and yet were still willing to help a neighbor defend against communist aggression. 7,420 soldiers served through five battalion combat team rotations between September 19, 1950 and May 13, 1955.

The KOREA CAMPAIGN MEDAL was awarded for service with the Philippine Expeditionary Force To Korea (PEFTOK) in or over Korea and adjacent waters. No minimum service period was specified.

The medal is bronze gilt. The obverse shows a Korean pagoda, three stars and the inscription "KOREAN CAMPAIGN". The reverse had the crossed flags of the United Nations over the Philippines on a mountain background over the Korean Taeguk symbol. The ribbon was silk moire. Earlier issues of the medal were cruder and had rougher textured ribbons. The later issues were more convex and had better detail. This medal exists in miniature. The example pictured was made by El Oro of Quezon City and the brooch is so named.

Small bronze stars could be affixed to the ribbon, one for each battle engagement. Every five engagements were signified by a silver star. Stars were arranged symetrically on the ribbon and ribbon bar.

The Philippines also awarded a wound medal and combat infantry badge.

The Philippine PRESIDENTIAL UNIT CITATION was given in the name of the President of the Republic. Philippine and allied armed forces units were eligible for this award in recognition for 'acts and services of exceptional gallantry and fidelity'.

The P.U.C. is a ribbon with vertical stripes of red/white/blue The ribbon has a gilt frame with palms similar to the U.S.A. issue citations. Bronze and silver stars indicate multiple awards, one silver star for every five awards.

The most highly decorated soldier of the Philippine Expeditionary Force is 1LT Benny Serrano of the 10th Battalion Combat Team. Two officers received the American Distinguished Service Cross posthumously for their part in the 10th B.C.T. efforts during the Imjin River battle of April. 1951.

U.N. #35943

Col. Abcede, commander of the 20th B.C.T., receives the ribbon of the R.O.K. Presidential Unit Citation. He is wearing a second award of the American Combat Infantry Badge.

HONORS AND AWARDS TO PEFTOK

UNIT

PHILIPPINES

PRESIDENTIAL UNIT CITATION

14th B.C.T.   March, 1954   For entire service period.

B Co. (less 2d Plt) and
Tank Co. of 10th B.C.T.   5 September, 1951   Yultong battle.

R.O.K.

PRESIDENTIAL UNIT CITATION

20 B.C.T.   11 JUN 52   Koyangdae and T-Bone Ridge
19 B.C.T.   JUL 52   Arsenal and Erie Outposts
14 B.C.T.   15 DEC 53   Satae-ri Valley and Paek-san

INDIVIDUAL AWARDS

PHILIPPINES

MEDAL FOR VALOR - 1   Wound Medal - 'over 300'
DISTINGUISHED CONDUCT STAR - 6
DISTINGUISHED SERVICE STAR - 1
GOLD CROSS MEDAL - 14
BRONZE CROSS MEDAL - 10
MILITARY MERIT MEDAL - 159

R.O.K.

ULCHI D.M.S.M. - 9   (includes 1 to Air Force)
CHUNGMU with GOLD STAR - 4
CHUNGMU with SILVER STAR - 14   (includes 1 to Air Force)
CHUNGMU - 6

U.S.A.

DISTINGUISHED SERVICE CROSS - 2   CPT YAP, Conrado   (posthumous award)
                                  1LT ARTIAGA, Jose   (posthumous award)
LEGION OF MERIT - 2
SILVER STAR - 8
BRONZE STAR with "V" - 5
BRONZE STAR - 58
AIR MEDAL - 5

MEDAL OF MERIT (Obv.)

SIGN OF MERIT (Obv.)

PLAQUE OF MERIT

BADGE OF MERIT

25th ANNIVERSARY COMMEMORATIVE MEDALLION

SWEDEN

The Swedish Red Cross provided a field hospital to the U.N. effort. Several of the awards of the Swedish Red Cross were given to those who served in Korea. These medals are still earned by members of expeditions such as the Biafra relief. The Swedish hospital was the first non- U.S.A. medical unit to arrive in Korea. The period of service was 23 SEP 50 - 10 APR 57.

Once hostilities ceased, the Swedish Field Hospital remained in Pusan until 1956 as a general hospital for civilians. Later, the Swedes, Danes, Norwegians and Koreans combined their resources and established the National Medical Center in Seoul to provide care and to train Korean health care personnel.

About 3,000 Swedes, men and women, served during the war on tours which varied from three months to two years. The standard contract was for six months, which could be extended, with some doctors and specialists serving only a three month contract.

The Swedish system of classifying medals is detailed in The Medal Collector, Vol.39 No.12; DEC 88. The following awards are semi official. They are approved by the King but are not awarded by him, rather, they are awarded by the Swedish Red Cross according to general permission of the King.

MEDAL OF MERIT OF Sw R.C./SVENSKA RÖDA KORSETS FÖRTJÄNSMEDALJ   This medal was instituted in 1911. The highest class was in gold and was 31mm in diameter. More common was the 24mm type or the even smaller silver version. The ribbon was blue/yellow/blue, the Swedish national colors.

The Medal of Merit in gold is awarded for 20 years of 'active and devoted service', while the silver medal is for recognition of ten - fifteen years. They are worn on the left breast.

Both the Medal and Sign of Merit are worn differently by female recipients. While the men wear theirs suspended by the ribbon, the ribbon is tied like a bow and worn as a brooch by the women.

SIGN OF MERIT OF Sw R.C.   This is a silver oval medal. The obverse is the Sw R.C. emblem with the Royal tricrown logo. The reverse is a rendering of the Good Samaritan. This too is worn on the left breast. It is awarded for five - ten years of service.

BADGE OF MERIT OF Sw R.C./SVENSKA RÖDA KORSETS FÖRTJÄNSETTECKEN   This badge was instituted in 1941. It exists only in one class. The ribbon is red, bordered white. The enamel red cross is bordered by gilt olive branches. It is worn as a brooch by female awardees. The recipients' name and address are on the reverse.

PLAQUE OF MERIT OF Sw R.C./SVENSKA RODA KORSETS FORTJANSPLAKETT This plaque was instituted in 1935. It measures 68mm x 100mm and is plated in gold, silver or bronze. The inscription tranlates as "FOR MERIT - SWEDISH RED CROSS".

This plaque can be awarded to non-members who have made significant service to the Swedish Red Cross.

25th ANNIVERSARY COMMEMORATIVE MEDALLION This non official medallion was offered for sale in 1975. It was 70mm and could be purchased in silver or bronze. It came with a wooden display stand. The illustration here is from the original sales brochure.

This medallion commemorates twentyfive years of Swedish involvement in U.N. operations worldwide, which began in Korea.

<u>HONORS AND AWARDS TO</u>
<u>SVENSKA KOREAAMBULANSEN</u>
<u>UNIT</u>
<u>R.O.K.</u>
P.U.C. - 3

<u>INDIVIDUAL</u>

Information concerning the numbers of awards made was not available. The Swedish awards were made on the basis of duty position as shown in the chart.

All personnel received the R.O.K. War Service Medal and the U.N. Korea medal in English. The United States Korean Campaign Medal was promised but never awarded.

Some senior personnel received the R.O.K. Ulchi, Chungmu and Wharang. In addition, the American Legion of Merit, Silver Star and Bronze Star medals were awarded in small numbers.

POSITION OF DUTY AT SVENSKA KOREA AMBULANSEN	MEDAL OF MERIT		SIGN OF MERIT
	GOLD	SILVER	
CHIEF DOCTOR (Regardless of length of service)	X		
OTHER MEDICAL DOCTORS, DENTISTS, PHARMACISTS, MILITARY COMPANY COMMANDERS, SUPPLY OFFICERS.			
4 - 5 MONTHS			X
6 MONTH MINIMUM		X	
OTHER OFFICERS OR THOSE WITH EQUAL STATUS			
4 - 7 MONTHS			X
8 MONTH MINIMUM		X	
ALL OTHERS, N.C.O.s, PRIVATES ETC.			
10 - 14 MONTHS			X
15 MONTH MINIMUM		X	

All others who did not receive the Medal or Sign of Merit were awarded the Swedish Red Cross Plaque of Merit.

Gunnar Nyby / Sweden Red Cross

Major Gunnar Nyby being presented the colors of the Swedish Red Cross Hospital in Stockholm before departure for Korea.

ROW 1: <u>KOREA CAMPAIGN MEDAL</u>; Obverse, Reverse. <u>KOREA CAMPAIGN</u> with <u>CITATION</u>.
ROW 2: <u>KOREA CAMPAIGN</u>; Miniature.
<u>KING'S MEDAL FOR SERVICE IN KOREA</u>; Obverse, Reverse.

THAILAND

The Royal Thai Forces in Korea were formed from the 1st Battalion, 21st Infantry Regiment. They served in Korea from November 7, 1950 until March 31, 1955. Today the 21st Regiment is the HM Queen Sirikit's Guard Unit. An air transport squadron and two corvettes also served. 6,180 Thai soldiers served in Korea before the cease fire.

The KOREAN CAMPAIGN MEDAL is a large silvered base metal medal. The ribbon hangs from a pin back bar which represents a Thai Field Marshal's baton. This bar is inscribed "Victory" in Thai script. The obverse shows a charging war elephant and the reverse is inscribed in Thai script which translates roughly as "We fight for Thailand's glory". This also exists as a finely detailed miniature. A gilt flame device on the ribbon is a citation device. The ribbon is U.N. blue with one narrow white stripe near each side.

10,376 campaign medals were awarded. 125 Thai troops died in Korea and 344 were wounded in action.

This medal, with different ribbons, had also been awarded for the 1941 Indochina war with France (red with white stripes near the edges) and World War Two (green with red and white stripes).

KING'S MEDAL FOR SERVICE IN KOREA   This is a Royal, not an official award. When the Siamese troops returned home, their King presented each soldier with a personal momento for their service. This was for wear on a chain or a fob. The medal is silver and has a ring suspender. The obverse is the monogram of King Rama IX. The reverse is Thai script which reads "Given by His Majesty to soldiers who served in Korea, 1954". This was awarded to the Thai Contingent to the U.N. Command until they were withdrawn in the mid 1960s.

ROYAL THAI FORCES IN KOREA

HONORS AND AWARDS

TO UNIT

THAILAND

UNIT CITATION - 1   15 AUG 54

R.O.K.

PRESIDENTIAL UNIT CITATION - 2   8 APR 54; For entire period of service.
20 MAY 54; For Hill 351, vicinity Kumwha, 14 -27 July, 1953.

INDIVIDUAL AWARDS

THAILAND

DISTINGUISHED SERVICE MEDAL - 37 [1]

R.O.K.

ULCHI D.M.S.M. - 7
CHUNGMU D.M.S.M. - 28   (including 1 to Royal Thai Navy)
WHARANG D.M.S.M. - 16
WAR SERVICE MEDAL - 3,142

BELGIUM

MEDAL FOR MILITARY MERIT - 6 [1]

---

(1) These awards are listed as described in the R.O.K. "History of the U.N. Forces". The correct titles of these awards isn't clear, this information had to survive three translations.

FROM U.S.A.

LEGION OF MERIT - 19		(including 3 to Royal Thai Air Force)
SILVER STAR - 13		1953 awards to 21st Regiment:

- 1LT SIRIBUM, Chaleru
- 1LT SOMROOP, Arkapol
- CPL CHOMSIRI, Tongyu
- CPL DOGTIEN, Prasert
- PFC DARACHAI, Aree
- PVT BHADNARI, Punya
- PVT BHROMIN, Yuhun
- PVT KICHPRACHOOM, Chuerak
- PVT KUANMOUNG, Prayoon

BRONZE STAR with "V" - 25

BRONZE STAR - 42 (includes 4 each to the Navy and the Air Force)

April, 1951 awards to 21st Regt.:
- 1LT PIRAPUL, Chotochong
- PFC SATIM, Kauetong
- PVT CHOUPOL, Siita

AIR MEDAL - 3 (to Royal Thai Air Force)

MEDAL OF FREEDOM - 2 to Thai Medical Service Detachment:
- DR KASEM, Chinprahas
- NURSE PRANHEE, Intuset

The third Thai rotation fought on Pork Chop Hill in November, 1952. One Legion of Merit, 12 Silver Stars and 26 Bronze Stars were awarded the Thai troops for this action. These awards are included in the above totals.

UNITED NATIONS KOREA MEDAL - TURKISH: Obverse, Reverse.

TURKEY

Troops of the Turkish Army Command Force received only the U.N. Korea Service Medal as a campaign medal. This brigade sized combined arms task force established a fearsome reputation for its offensive capability and front line conduct. 1st Brigade served from October 18, 1950 until September 1, 1951. 2d Brigade arrived on September 1, 1951; 3d Brigade on July 30, 1952 and 4th Brigade served from September 4, 1953 until May 1954. Exclusive of the 4th Brigade (which arrived after the cease fire), 14,936 Turkish soldiers served in Korea.

In 1923, the Turkish Republic outlawed all decorations beyond those awarded for the War of Independence. Consequently, Turkey awarded no campaign medal. The U.N. Korea Service Medal was issued "as a momento" by the Turkish Military Council but wear of the medal was banned. Awardees would sometimes wear them under their lapel. Turks would replace the issue ribbon with a plain red one. The U.N. colors are also those of Greece and are therefore anathematic to a Turk. In 1964, Turkish veterans were said to be returning their U.N. Korea Medals as a result of the U.N. intervention in Cyprus.

22,500 of the 33,696 Turkish U.N. Korea Medals were struck by the Administration Des Monnaies et Medailles in Paris, France.

Three Turks received the American Distinguished Service Cross. At least fifteen Turks were decorated with American Silver Star and Bronze Star medals for their part in the battles near Kunu-Ri in November, 1950.

U.S.A. DISTINGUISHED SERVICE CROSS TO TURKISH ARMY
for actions on 28 - 29 May, 1953.

CPT SUKAN, Sinasi	D.A. G.O. 43, 1955	
1LT URER, Rustu	D.A. G.O. 17, 1954;	Posthumous award.
SGT ERGIN, Mehmet	D.A. G.O. 43, 1955	

KOREA MEDAL   Reverse.   (James W. Lang)   KOREA MEDAL, Miniature, Reverse.

Mounted Korea trio to S.A.A.F. airman.
Left to Right: KOREA MEDAL;   U.N. KOREA MEDAL;   R.O.K. WAR SERVICE MEDAL.

UNION OF SOUTH AFRICA

No.2 Squadron, South African Air Force, served in Korea from November 16, 1950 until October 29, 1953. The "Cheetah" Squadron operated in the close air support role under the U.S. 18th Fighter-Bomber Wing. The Cheetahs earned an excellent reputation for their courage and skill while flying the F-51 Mustang and F-86 Sabrejet. The intensity of their operations is illustrated by their loss of 74 of the 95 mustangs flown by the squadron. The members were hand picked, most of the initial members having served in World War Two. Many of the officers had already been decorated.

243 Officers and 545 Other Ranks of the Air Force served in Korea, nine officers having a second tour. 23 officers and 15 other ranks from the Army also served. Ten officer positions were reserved for South Africans at the Commonwealth Division headquarters. 34 pilots and two ground crew died and seven prisoners of war were returned. Of 846 South Africans who served in Korea, 797 received the Korea Medal.

The eligibility dates for the Korea Medal were September 19, 1950 to July 27, 1953. Qualification required one day service on the strength of an active unit or thirty days total for official tours and inspections.

The medals are named in impressed block capitals. The South Africans received the english language U.N. Korea Medal.

The medal is cupro-nickel and it's design is similar to that of British medals. A miniature was also produced.

Further details on the recipients can be found in the "South Africa Korea Roll" by Colin Owen. This is currently out of print but shows up on dealers lists, especially in the U.K.. There are four names missing from this roll that have since been confirmed. One of these is J.D.S. SNYDERS, P16322.

HONORS AND AWARDS

UNIT

R.O.K.

PRESIDENTIAL UNIT CITATION - No.2 Squadron, S.A.A.F.

U.S.A.

PRESIDENTIAL UNIT CITATION - No.2 Squadron, S.A.A.F.

HONORS AND AWARDS - con't

INDIVIDUAL

SOUTH AFRICA / COMMONWEALTH

M.B.E. - 2

M.I.D. - 2

KOREA MEDAL - 797

U.S.A.

LEGION OF MERIT - 3

DISTINGUISHED FLYING CROSS - 50   1 OAK LEAF CLUSTER (denotes second award)

SILVER STAR - 2

BRONZE STAR - 40

SOLDIERS MEDAL - 1

AIR MEDAL - 176   (152 OAK LEAF CLUSTERS)

"Those crazy bastards...the Hall of Fame doesn't possess any greater men than those who flew that day..." (Letter to the squadron from a U.S. Marine.)

R.O.K.

ULCHI D.M.S.M. w/SILVER STAR - 2

ULCHI D.M.S.M. - 4

CHUNGMU D.M.S.M. w/GOLD STAR - 5

CHUNGMU D.M.S.M. w/SILVER STAR - 6

WHARANG D.M.S.M. w/GOLD STAR - 2

WHARANG D.M.S.M. w/SILVER STAR - 2

WAR SERVICE MEDAL - 818

TAEGUK w/GOLD STAR - 1   (To the South African Unknown Airman)

UNION OF SOVIET SOCIALIST REPUBLICS

Recent declassifications of material by western and the Soviet governments has revealed a heretofore unknown (to the west) level of active Soviet participation in the war.

Upwards of 70,000 members of the Soviet armed forces served on or in support of Korean War operations. Most belonged to the Air Defense Forces (P.V.O.) and manned anti-aircraft defenses protecting the Manchurian airfields. One division of MIG-15 jet fighters flew alongside their Korean and Chinese allies in direct combat against U.N. forces. At least twelve divisions were rotated through. Soviet advisors and liason officers also served on the ground, primarily with the North Koreans. The Soviets have also admitted to an "anti-decontamination medical unit" near Pyongyang.

At least twentyone Soviet pilots received the highest military decoration, "Hero of the Soviet Union". Two of these were posthumous. Over fourteen Red Air Force pilots reached 'ace' status with five or more kills. The highest total was attained by Yevgeny Pepelaev with 23 kills.

GOLD STAR / HERO OF THE SOVIET UNION - 21+   COL SMORTZKOW, Alexander P.*

* Colonel Smortzkow commanded the 18th Aviation Regiment of MIG-15 fighters. He claims twelve 'kills' over allied aircraft; seven American and five Australian.

ROW 1:   KOREA MEDAL, Type II.   PAIR: KOREA MEDAL, Type I; U.N. KOREA.

ROW 2:   KOREA MEDAL, Miniature, Type I.   KOREA MEDAL, CANADA/Type II
KOREA MEDAL, Reverse, all types.

ROW 3:   Palm badge for MENTION IN DISPATCHES.
United States PRESIDENTIAL UNIT CITATION. These are the British made embroidered versions. The red background (left) is for the dress uniform while the olive background is for the No.2 service uniform.

UNITED KINGDOM AND COMMONWEALTH
"THE QUEEN'S KOREA"

The KOREA MEDAL was awarded by the governments of the United Kingdom, Australia, Canada and New Zealand to those servicemembers who served in the Korean theater. The medal was approved by King George VI in 1951 and was designed by Mary Gillick, G.B.E. (obverse) and E. Carter Preston (reverse).

The obverse shows Queen Elizabeth II facing to her left while the reverse shows Hercules fending off the many headed Hydra, which presumably represents communism. The medal was struck with three types of obverse. Each differs in the legend:

Type I: ELIZABETH II DEI GRA:BRITT: OMN:REGINA F:D +
Type II: ELIZABETH II DEI :GRATIA:REGINA F:D +   (Type II deletes "BRITT OMN")
Type III: ELIZABETH II DEI GRATIA REGINA   CANADA ("CANADA" appears below the bust)

The medal is made of cupro-nickel, except for Canadian issues, which are silver.

British medals are impressed in thin capitals. Naming is service number; rank; name and unit. Australian, Canadian and some New Zealand medals have service number and name only. The Commonwealth issues are impressed with larger capitals.

Those so entitled wear the bronze oak leaf signifying a Mention in Dispatches centered on the ribbon.

Award criteria were the same for all four countries but varied with the branch of service. Opening and closing dates are July 2, 1950 until July 27, 1953, inclusive.

ARMY: 1 day in country on unit strength.
NAVY: 28 days afloat in operational waters; 1 day shore duty; 1 sortie over Korea or adjacent waters.
AIR FORCE: 1 sortie over Korea or adjacent waters; 1 day on land or 28 days afloat with the Navy.

Official visits totaling thirty or more days also qualified. Service terminated by wounds, sickness or death still qualified. It was possible to earn the U.N. Korea Medal without the Queen's Korea Medal due to the longer eligibility period of the former.

The blue of the ribbon is from the U.N. flag while yellow is the traditional British color used with medals for service in the Orient.

Due to privacy regulations, the Korea medals are difficult to research. There are some useful sources however. There have recently been published updated rolls for British prisoners of war, U.K. and Commonwealth Mentions-in Dispatches and a Gloster Imjin roll. The Korea specific regimental histories that have been published contain rolls of honor, list P.O.W.s and casualties and mention names of all ranks. Units that have published their Korean War histories are the Royal Ulster Rifles, the Argyle & Sutherland Highlanders, the King's Own Scottish Borderers and 41 Commando, Royal Marines.

Many British soldiers served in Korea as attachments to other regiments. The Korea Medal is usually named to the unit with which the soldier served. Gallantry awards, however, are named to the soldiers parent unit. Lest matters be too easy, there are exceptions to how the Korea Medals are named...

BRITISH LINE REGIMENTS IN KOREA

ARMOR

C SQD, 7 ROYAL TANK REGIMENT	(7 RTR)	NOV 50 - OCT 51
8 KING'S ROYAL IRISH HUSSARS	(8 HUSSARS)	NOV 50 - NOV 51
5 ROYAL INNISKILLING DRAGOON GUARDS	(5 INNIS DG)	DEC 51 - DEC 52
1 ROYAL TANK REGIMENT	(1 R TKS)	DEC 52 - DEC 53

INFANTRY

1 BN, MIDDLESEX REGIMENT	(MIDDLESEX)	AUG 50 - MAY 51
1 BN, ARGYLE & SUTHERLAND HIGHLANDERS	(A SH)	AUG 50 - APR 51
1 BN, ROYAL NORTHUMBERLAND FUSILIERS	(RNF)	NOV 50 - OCT 51
1 BN, GLOUCESTERSHIRE REGIMENT	(GLOSTER)	NOV 50 - NOV 51
1 BN, ROYAL ULSTER RIFLES	(RUR)	NOV 50 - OCT 51
1 BN, KING'S OWN SCOTTISH BORDERERS	(KOSB)	APR 51 - AUG 52
1 BN, KING'S SHROPSHIRE LIGHT INFANTRY	(KSLI)	MAY 51 - SEP 52
1 BN, ROYAL NORFOLK REGIMENT	(NORFOLK)	OCT 51 - SEP 52
1 BN, LEICESTERSHIRE REGIMENT	(LEICESTER)	OCT 51 - JUN 52
1 BN, THE WELCH REGIMENT	(WELCH)	NOV 51 - NOV 52
1 BN, BLACK WATCH (ROYAL HIGHLAND REGIMENT)	(BW)	JUN 52 - JUL 53
1 BN, ROYAL FUSILIERS	(RF)	AUG 52 - AUG 53
1 BN, DURHAM LIGHT INFANTRY	(DLI)	SEP 52 - SEP 53
1 BN, THE KING'S REGIMENT	(KINGS)	SEP 52 - OCT 53
1 BN, DUKE OF WELLINGTON'S REGIMENT	(DWR)	SEP 52 - OCT 53
1 BN, THE ROYAL SCOTS	(R SCOT)	JUL 53 - MAY 54

British Information Services via United Nations

The commander of the Eighth Army, LTG Van Fleet, pins the U.S. Presidential Unit Citation on SGM Thomas Blackford of the 1st Bn., Gloucestershire Regiment. The survivors of the famous Imjin River battle were decorated in May, 1951.

HONORS AND AWARDS TO BRITISH TROOPS

VICTORIA CROSS

*MAJ KENNETH MUIR	1 ARGYLE & SUTHERLAND HIGHLANDERS	1 MAY 51	KIA
LTC JOSEPH P. CARNE	1 GLOUCESTERSHIRE REGIMENT	27 NOV 53	MIA/POW
* LT K.P.E. CURTIS	D.C.L.I. Attd: 1 GLOUCESTERSHIRE	1 DEC 53	KIA
PTE WILLIAM SPEAKMAN	BLACK WATCH Attd: 1 K.O.S.B.	28 DEC 51	WIA

*Posthumous award. Dates are those of the London Gazette notification.

ABOVE: COLONEL J.P. CARNE V.C., D.S.O.

This is his medal group as displayed in the National Army Museum, London, in 1989. The medals are held by the Gloucestershire Regimental Museum. Colonel Carne's V.C. action also resulted in the award of the United State's second highest honor, the Distinguished Service Cross.

OPPOSITE: MAJOR KENNETH MUIR V.C.

Major Muir was killed during his V.C. action. He is buried in the U.N. Cemetary at Pusan, Korea. His medals are at Stirling Castle in the Regimental Museum of the Argyl & Sutherland Highlanders. His awards also include the American Distinguished Service Cross. Like the medals to Sergeant Speakman, Major Muir's medals reflect service in combat on campaigns spanning twenty years.

Argyll & Sutherland
Highlanders Regimental
Museum

MAJOR KENNETH MUIR V.C.
1st BN, ARGYLL & SUTHERLAND HIGHLANDERS

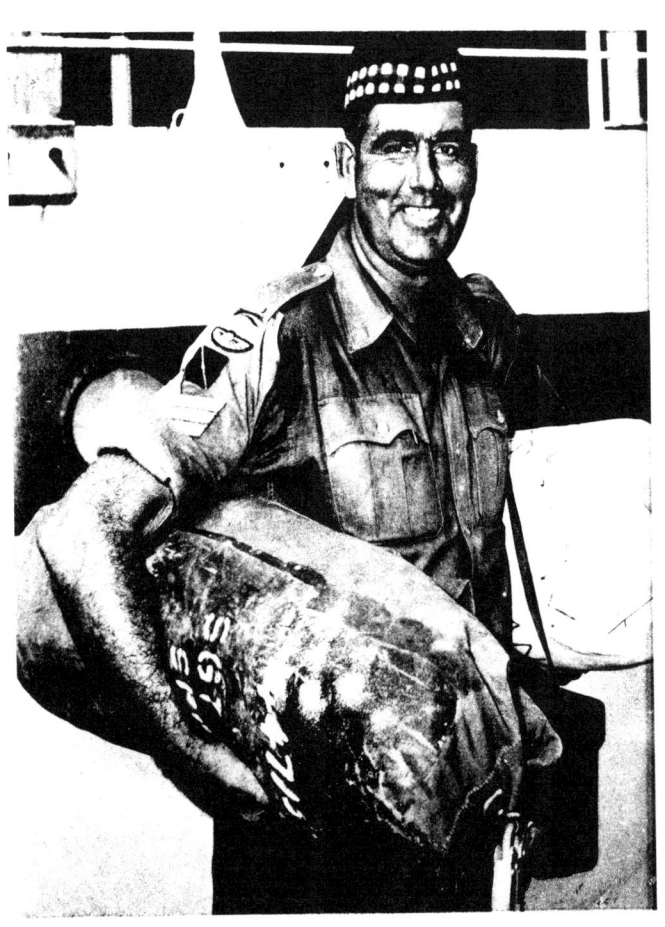

SERGEANT WILLIAM SPEAKMAN V.C.

The then Private Speakman defended his company from a heavy Chinese assault by making repeated counter-attacks into the enemy ranks despite his wounds. His later service included a tour with the famous 22 Special Air Service Regiment. His medals are at the Scottish United Services Museum at Edinburgh Castle.

Top: Stephen Wood / S.U.S.M. #A2087
Left: King's Own Scottish Borderers Museum

Lieutenant Phillip Kenneth Edward Curtis, V.C.

Awarded the Victoria Cross posthumously for his magnificent conduct throughout the bitter battle of the Imjin River, on the night of April 22nd 23rd, 1951

Duke of Cornwall's Light Infantry Museum

LT Curtis' medals are on display in the museum of the Duke of Cornwall's Light Infantry. They are the Victoria Cross; War Medal (1939 - 1945); Korea Medal and the United Nations Korea Medal. Lt Curtis V.C. is buried in the United Nations Cemetary in Pusan, Korea.

GEORGE CROSS

*40378 2/LT T.E. WATERS   WEST YORKS Attd: 1 GLOUCESTERSHIRE   13 MAY 54   KIA
FUSILIER D.G. KINNE   1 ROYAL NORTHUMBERLAND FUSILIERS   13 MAY 54   POW

2/LT T.E. WATERS G.C.

These are 2/Lt Water's medals as displayed at the National Army Museum in 1989. They are in the Gloucestershire Regimental Museum. The George Cross recipients both received their awards for their conduct in the prisoner of war camps. Both were captured during the Imjin River battle of April, 1951.

Fusilier Derek Kinne GC, 1st Bn. Royal Northumberland Fusiliers is shown here on the day of his investiture at Buckingham Palace on 6th July 1954.
His gallantry as a POW of the Chinese Communists in Korea was an epic of blazing courage and almost incredible endurance.

D.G. Kinne G.C. via A. Cunningham-Boothe

DISTINGUISHED SERVICE ORDER

LTC A.M. MAN, OBE	1 MIDDLESEX		12 DEC 50
LTC G.L. NEILSON	1 A & SH		12 DEC 50
MAJ R.M. PRATT	1 R.N.F.		17 APR 51
MAJ J.K.H. SHAW, MC	1 R.U.R.		17 APR 51
A/LTC D.B. DRYSDALE, MBE	41 IND CDO, R.M.		18 MAY 51
MAJ P.H. HUTH, MC	8 K.R.I.H.		1 JUN 51
MAJ H.J. WINN, MC	1 R.N.F.		29 JUN 51
MAJ H.M. GAFFIKIN	1 R.U.R.		10 JUL 51
MAJ C.M. MITCHELL	1 R.N.F.		10 JUL 51
LTC JOSEPH P. CARNE	1 GLOSTER		13 JUL 51
LTC K.O.N. FOSTER	1 R.N.F.		13 JUL 51
BRIG. THOMAS BRODIE, CBE	29 INF BDE		7 SEP 51
CPT A.H. FARRAR-HOCKLEY	1 GLOSTER		8 DEC 53
MAJ E.D. HARDING	1 GLOSTER		8 DEC 53
CPT E.D.G. SHULDHAM	41 IND CDO, R.M.		3 SEP 52
MAJ W.G.O. BUTLER, MC	8 K.R.I.H.		30 NOV 51
MAJ W.J. COTTLE	1 K.S.L.I.		30 NOV 51
LTC J.F.M. MACDONALD, OBE	1 K.O.S.B.		30 NOV 51
MAJ P.F. St C. HARRISON	1 K.O.S.B.		28 DEC 51
2/LT W. PURVES	1 K.O.S.B.		28 DEC 51*
MAJ P.H.V. de CLERMONT	8 K.R.I.H.		29 APR 52
MAJ R.C. ROBERTSON-MACLEOD, MC	1 K.O.S.B.		29 APR 52
MAJ T.J. JACKSON	1 WELCH		29 AUG 52
LTC P.N.M. MOORE, DSO MC	28 FLD REGT, RA	2d BAR	10 OCT 52
MAJ D.G.M. FLETCHER	28 FLD REGT, RA		10 OCT 52
LTC V.W. BARLOW, DSO OBE	1 K.S.L.I.	BAR	10 OCT 52
LTC G.E.P. HUTCHINS	1 ROYAL LEICESTERS		10 OCT 52
LTC D.H. TADMAN, OBE	1 K.O.S.B.		10 OCT 52
MAJ A.D.H. IRWIN, MC	1 BLACK WATCH		9 JAN 53
MAJ B.D. CHAPMAN	1 ROYAL NORFOLK		24 APR 53
LTC H.H. DEANE	1 WELCH		24 APR 53
MAJ A.G. ROBERTS	1 WELCH		24 APR 53
MAJ R.A. PONT	14 FLD REGT, RA		24 APR 53
MAJ J.M.H. HAILES	1093 IND AOP FLT, RA		24 APR 53
LTC DAVID M.C. ROSE, DSO	1 BLACK WATCH	BAR	1 JUN 53

*William Purves won his D.S.O. as a Subaltern in the Speakman V.C. action.

D.S.O. (con't)

LTC F.R. St P. BUNBURY D.S.O.	1 D.W.R.	BAR	7 JUL 53
MAJ L.F.H. KERSHAW	1 D.W.R.		7 JUL 53
LTC P.J. JEFFREYS D.S.O., O.B.E.	1 D.L.I.	BAR	8 DEC 53
LTG T.G. BRENNAN C.B.E.	20 FLD REGT, R.A.		8 DEC 53
BRIG D.A. KENDREW C.B.E., D.S.O.	29 INF BDE	3d BAR	8 DEC 53
MG M.M.A.R. WEST C.B., D.S.O.	1 COMMONWEALTH DIV	2d BAR	8 DEC 53

MENTION IN DISPATCHES

Over 1,300 personnel from the United Kingdom and Commonwealth were Mentioned in Dispatches. A Mention in Dispatches is signified by a bronze oak leaf affixed to the ribbon and ribbon bar of the Korea Medal. For a roll of M.I.D.s for Korea, refer to "KOREA 1950 - 1953; UNITED KINGDOM AND COMMONWEALTH PERSONNEL MENTIONED IN DISPATCHES" by Peter Dyke.

77 M.I.D.s were awarded to non-Commonwealth personnel.

The bronze oak leaf also denotes a post 1945 award of the King's or Queen's Commendation for Brave Conduct in the Air.

The post 1945 M.I.D. emblem differs slightly in shape from earlier issues.

HONORS AND AWARDS TO THE BRITISH FORCES

The available references frequently disagree on the totals of awards made for Korean actions. This compilation is of awards to British troops, including those attached to Commonwealth forces. Award totals in this book to Commonwealth forces are to individuals who were members of Commonwealth forces. This compilation will not be the last word on the subject.

Essential to the researcher is the roll of British and Commonwealth awards and decorations for Korea compiled by Mr Ashley Cunningham-Boothe of the British Korea Veterans Association. See "MARKS OF COURAGE", Korvet Publishing, Warwickshire, U.K. "The 38th PARALLEL" by Peter Gaston, Glasgow, 1976, contains a handy, if less complete, roll of awards to the British Army.

Issues of British gallantry awards during this period will include both GVIR and EIIR coinages.

The King's Own Scottish Borderers won three Distinguished Conduct Medals in Korea, more than any other British regiment. However, the widely claimed D.C.M. to SGT J. Moss of the regiment is in error as the award was never made. Courtesy Mr Cunningham-Boothe who helped clear up this claim with the regiment.

K.I.

MILITARY CROSS, 1951
Second type GVIR coinage, dated 1951.

The Military Cross is a gallantry award primarily for junior officers. It is engraved with the year the award was made and is not named unless done so by the recipient.

HONORS AND AWARDS

BRITISH ARMY

VICTORIA CROSS - 4	GEORGE CROSS - 2
K.B.E. - 1	C.B.E. - 4
O.B.E. - 29	M.B.E. - 80
DISTINGUISHED SERVICE ORDER - 32	D.S.O. 1st BAR - 4
D.S.O. 2d BAR - 2	D.S.O. 3d BAR - 1
DISTINGUISHED SERVICE CROSS - 11	D.S.C. 1st BAR - 3
DISTINGUISHED CONDUCT MEDAL - 13	
BRITISH EMPIRE MEDAL - 30	GEORGE MEDAL - 3
MILITARY CROSS - 107	M.C. 1st BAR - 7 (6)
DISTINGUISHED FLYING CROSS - 12	DISTINGUISHED FLYING MEDAL - 2
MILITARY MEDAL - 111	M.M. 1st BAR - 1
AIR FORCE MEDAL - 1	MENTION IN DISPATCHES - 571

ROYAL NAVY

K.B.E. - 1	C.B.E. - 6
O.B.E. - 17	M.B.E. - 27
BRITISH EMPIRE MEDAL - 54	DISTINGUISHED SERVICE ORDER - 16
D.S.O. 1st BAR - 3	D.S.O. 2d BAR - 2
DISTINGUISHED SERVICE CROSS - 42	D.S.C. 1st BAR - 17
D.S.C. 2d BAR - 2	DISTINGUISHED SERVICE MEDAL - 20
D.S.M. 1st BAR - 1	

ROYAL MARINES

DISTINGUISHED SERVICE ORDER - 2	DISTINGUISHED SERVICE CROSS - 3
BRITISH EMPIRE MEDAL - 1	MILITARY CROSS - 3
DISTINGUISHED SERVICE MEDAL -	MILITARY MEDAL - 9

ROYAL AIR FORCE

O.B.E. - 1	BRITISH EMPIRE MEDAL - 1
DISTINGUISHED FLYING CROSS - 22	D.F.C. 1st BAR - 3
DISTINGUISHED FLYING MEDAL - 8	

AMERICAN AWARDS TO BRITISH FORCES

UNIT AWARDS

PRESIDENTIAL UNIT CITATION: 1 BN. GLOUCESTERSHIRE REGIMENT
C TROOP, 170 IND. MORTAR BATTERY, R.A.
FOR SOLMA-RI / IMJIN RIVER   22 - 25 APRIL, 1951

NAVAL PRESIDENTIAL UNIT CITATION: 41 COMMANDO, ROYAL MARINES
FOR CHOSIN RESERVOIR,   NOVEMBER - DECEMBER 1950

This award was not presented until 1957 as U.S. Navy regulations didn't originally allow bestowal upon foreign forces.

INDIVIDUAL AWARDS

BRITISH ARMY
DISTINGUISHED SERVICE CROSS - 2
LEGION OF MERIT - 14 [1]
SILVER STAR - 14
DISTINGUISHED FLYING CROSS - 4
BRONZE STAR with "V" - 7
BRONZE STAR - 38
AIR MEDAL - 12   1st Oak Leaf Cluster

ROYAL AIR FORCE [5]
LEGION OF MERIT - 1
DISTINGUISHED FLYING CROSS - 12
BRONZE STAR - 5
AIR MEDAL - 35 [2]

ROYAL MARINES
LEGION OF MERIT - 1
SILVER STAR - 4   1st OLC
BRONZE STAR - 11 [3]

ROYAL NAVY
LEGION OF MERIT - 29
SILVER STAR - 1
BRONZE STAR with "V" - 2
BRONZE STAR - 5
AIR MEDAL - 1 [4]

---

1. The Silver Star medals to General Brodie and General Coad were withdrawn and replaced with higher awards of the Legion of Merit.

2. This includes four awards to R.A.F. pilots attached to the Royal Australian Air Force in Korea. Courtesy William R. Westlake who helped clarify much data on U.S. awards to the Commonwealth.

3. This figure includes Bronze Stars with "V".

4. This Air Medal was to a Fleet Air Arm officer.

5. The majority of R.A.F. personnel in Korea flew in air observation post flights as part of the Commonwealth Division or attached to American or Australian Air Force squadrons.

FRENCH AWARDS TO BRITISH FORCES

CROIX DE GUERRE DES T.O.E. - 5
- BRIG G.P. GREGSON — 1 COMWEL DIV
- LTC T.G. BRENNAN — ROYAL ARTILLERY
- MAJ F.S.G. SHORE — R.A.
- CPT J.G. MORGAN — R.A.
- CPT H. FAIRGRAVE — R.A.

These awards were not recognized by the British authorities until 1991. The presentation finally occurred at the French Embassy in London on March 28, 1991. The widow of Brigadier Gregson accepted his award.

The awards are by original authority of Order No.108, BF-ONU, LTC De Germiny, Commander, October 19, 1953.

Dr Peter Farrar via A. Cunningham-Boothe

PRESENTATION OF THE CROIX DE GUERRE, MARCH 28, 1991.

From front, L to R: Maj Scott SHORE; COL Geoffrey BRENNAN; MRS GREGSON; LTCOL Hugh FAIRGRAVE; MAJ John MORGAN.

Back: COL Georges POUPARD; President, French Korean Veteran's Association, who helped make this long overdue presentation possible.

ROW 1: Ribbon bars: Korea Service Medal; Merchant Marine Korea Service, on the left is the original award, pre 1992.

ROW 2: <u>KOREA SERVICE MEDAL</u>; miniature; Obverse, Reverse.
<u>MERCHANT MARINE KOREAN SERVICE MEDAL</u>; Obverse, minature reverse.

ROW 3: <u>ARMY OF OCCUPATION</u> with <u>KOREA</u> bar; <u>NATIONAL DEFENSE SERVICE MEDAL</u>; Obverse, reverse. <u>ARMED FORCES EXPEDITIONARY MEDAL</u>; Obverse.

ROW 4: <u>OAK LEAF CLUSTER</u> & <u>BRONZE STAR DEVICE</u> to denote repeat medal awards. <u>COMBAT INFANTRY BADGE</u>; <u>COMBAT MEDIC BADGE</u>.

UNITED STATES OF AMERICA
FEDERAL MEDALS & BADGES

KOREAN SERVICE MEDAL   Authorized by Executive Order No. 10179 to members of the U.S. Armed Forces. No civilians were eligible. Qualifying dates are June 27, 1950 to July 27, 1954. Individuals must have served in the Korean theater for thirty consecutive days or sixty non-consecutive days. Service terminated by wounds or death also qualified. Bronze or silver stars were worn on the medal ribbon or ribbon bar for designated campaigns. One silver star represented five campaigns, the bronze stars stood for one each. Personnel stationed outside of Korea but still in the theater who directly supported Korean operations, such as Air Force groundcrew, were also eligible.

NATIONAL DEFENSE SERVICE MEDAL   Authorized on April 22, 1953 by Executive Order No. 10486. All those who served in all components of the U.S. Armed Forces, not just those in Korea, between June 27, 1950 and July 27, 1959 qualified. This was usually awarded after sixty days of service, which corresponded to the completion of recruit training for many recipients, hence the sobriquet "the mop sloping medal". Reserve and National Guard personnel who were not activated generally did not receive the N.D.S.M. because of the sixty days active duty requirement. Period issues are matte bronze and are of generally higher quality than later issues. Later service during the Vietnam and Southwest Asia qualifying periods is recognized by a small oak leaf cluster (Army) or bronze star (all other services) on the medal ribbon or ribbon bar.

ARMY OF OCCUPATION MEDAL   Along with the 'JAPAN' and 'GERMANY' awards, this medal was awarded for service with Army and Air Force units and the Military Assistance and Advisory Group (MAAG) in Korea between September 3, 1945 and June 29, 1949 when the last U.S. occupation troops left Korea. The M.A.A.G. remained but no longer qualified for this medal. It was authorized by War Department General Orders No.32 of 1946 for Army and (Army) Air Force personnel. An unofficial bar 'KOREA' exists. This bar would be worn on the ribbon and ribbon bar.

NAVY OCCUPATION SERVICE MEDAL   This medal was authorized by Navy Department G.O. No.255 of January 28, 1948. Bars 'EUROPE' and 'ASIA' were authorized. The 'ASIA' bar was awarded to personnel of the Navy, Marine Corps and Coast Guard who served in the "Asiatic and Pacific area" between September 2, 1945 and April 27, 1952. This would have included Korea between 1945 and the 1949 pullout. Service in Japan and Okinawa counted until the closing date. This medal has differing reverses for the "UNITED STATES NAVY" and "UNITED STATES MARINES".

PRISONER OF WAR SERVICE MEDAL   This medal was established in 1986 by an act of Congress and signed into law by President Reagan. Any member of the U.S. Armed Forces who was a prisoner of war after April 5, 1917 "while engaged in action against an enemy of the United States or while serving with friendly forces engaged in armed conflict" was eligible. Recipients conduct while in captivity must have been honorable. Posthumous awards are made to the next of kin. Awards for service previous to 1986 must be requested by the recipient or next of kin. Because of this, awards to Korean War prisoners of war are scarce and will probably remain so. 7,000 Americans were held as prisoners of war in Korea. Only 3,450 were returned, 389 known P.O.W.s remain unaccounted for.

ARMED FORCES EXPEDITIONARY MEDAL   This medal was not authorized in connection with the 1950 - 1953 war but since a peace treaty never officialy ended the war, this medal is included here as its later award was a direct consequence of the 1950 - 1953 war. The A.F.E.M. was authorized for service in Korea from October 1, 1966 to June 30, 1974. During much of this period there was frequent combat on the Demilitarized Zone and numerous infiltration attempts by North Korean forces throughout the Republic of Korea. Some Combat Infantry Badges were awarded on the D.M.Z. and there were American casualties. Repeat tours in this theater did not qualify for second awards of the A.F.E.M.. Oak leaves or stars on the ribbon or ribbon bar signify awards from other qualifying operations.

COMBAT INFANTRY BADGE   The C.I.B. was instituted during World War Two as a means of recognition of the horrid and miserable lot of the combat infantry soldier. Award of this badge required thirty days (waiverable) service in a combat zone with at least one enemy engagement. The soldier had to hold an infantry occupational specialty and be serving in an infantry designated slot in an infantry unit (regiment or below) to be eligible. This was an Army award. The C.I.B. was also awarded to some members of allied units who otherwise qualified. Repeat tours in Korea did not qualify for a second award. Infantrymen who held a C.I.B. for W.W.2 service were recognized by a star above the badge between the ends of the wreaths. Service ended by death, wounds or illness would qualify.

COMBAT MEDIC BADGE   The C.M.B. is comparable to the C.I.B.. As the medics assigned to the front line combat units were technically "noncombatants", they were ineligible for the C.I.B.. Prerequisites were comparable to the C.I.B. except that the soldier had to be a medic serving in a combat arms unit.

Medical personnel from the other services were eligible if they were attached to infantry units and otherwise qualified. As with the C.I.B., World War Two awards had a star added to indicate a Korean award.

Later service in Vietnam resulted in awards of the C.I.B./C.M.B. with a star or a second star, as appropriate. The two star triple awards were sometimes known as "perfect attendance awards".

The C.I.B./C.M.B. was made of silver or 1/20th silver filled cupro-nickel. Attachment was with brooch type pins or later, with clutch back pins. The background of the C.I.B. was infantry blue enamel. Half size miniature versions exist for wear on formal uniforms. Subdued and embroidered versions didn't appear until the 1960s. Both badges could be worn on all uniforms.

U.S. MERCHANT MARINE

The U.S. Merchant Marine established a series of gallantry awards and campaign bars for World War Two and postwar service. Most of these correspond to a military award or service medal.

The KOREA SERVICE RIBBON BAR was awarded to Masters, Officers and crew members of U.S. merchant vessels for service in Korean waters between June 30, 1950 and September 30, 1953. It was authorized by an Act of Congress on June 24, 1956 (Public Law 759, 84th Congress) and was awarded by the Merchant Marine Awards Committee on December 14, 1956. Initially, the Korean War Service Bar existed as a ribbon bar only. It was issued with a wallet size certificate. Over 900 awards had been issued by 1983.

KOREA SERVICE MEDAL The Merchant Marine Decorations and Medals Act of May 30, 1988, authorized the creation of medals to correspond to the existing campaign ribbon bars. These became available in 1992. The reverse design is common to the series, that being the U.S.M.M. shield and anchor with the words "UNITED STATES MERCHANT MARINE". The obverse is the Korean Tori Gate with a Taeguk centered, the entire design being bordered by a chain. The miniature is one half size and has a clutch back attachment. The new ribbon lacks the watered edges between the colors.

The GALLANT SHIP MEDALLION AND CITATION PLAQUE was only awarded to one ship during this period. Officers and crew are entitled to wear the GALLANT SHIP CITATION RIBBON. This is an aquamarine ribbon with each end bordered white. A silver seahorse is affixed to the ribbon.

ROW 1: VERMONT NATIONAL DEFENSE MEDAL; P.R.N.G. COMBAT SERVICE MEDAL; CHELSEA / NORTH CHELSEA, MA. KOREA MEDAL.

ROW 2: OKLAHOMA CROSS OF VALOR; PUERTO RICO MEDAL OF HONOR FOR KILLED IN ACTION; CALIFORNIA FEDERAL SERVICE RIBBON.

UNITED STATES - STATE MEDALS

Illustrations in this section are provided only for those awards that are specific to Korea but all of these medals and ribbons were awarded in connection with Korean War service. For complete coverage of state military service awards, see "STATE MEDALS FOR WAR SERVICE" by Douglas Boyce.

CALIFORNIA FEDERAL SERVICE RIBBON   Awarded to California National Guard members who were called into active federal service during W.W.2, Korea, Vietnam and the Southwest Asia service periods. One of the two National Guard divisions to see Korean combat was the California based 40th Infantry Division.

OKLAHOMA CROSS OF VALOR   Awarded to state residents who became prisoners of war. Approximately 600 have been awarded over three wars. The Oklahoma based 45th Infantry Division was the other National Guard division to fight in Korea.

PUERTO RICO NATIONAL GUARD COMBAT SERVICE MEDAL   Awarded to all P.R.N.G. and P.R.A.N.G. members who served in combat at brigade/regimental level or below. The reverse reads "WAR SERVICE" due to the manufacturer's mistake. It was supposed to read "COMBAT SERVICE".

PUERTO RICO NATIONAL GUARD MEDAL FOR WOUNDED IN ACTION   Eligibility included those in P.R.N.G. units in Korea who were wounded while serving with that unit. This medal would be in addition to the Purple Heart.

PUERTO RICO MEDAL OF HONOR FOR KILLED IN ACTION   Presented to the next of kin of Puerto Ricans killed in action in Korea. 743 Puerto Ricans met this fate. All are eligible, regardless of service component. The servicemember's rank, name, and date of death are engraved on the reverse.

PUERTO RICO WAR SERVICE RIBBON   To P.R.N.G. members who served during W.W.2 or Korea. Contrary to common belief, the Puerto Rican based and manned 65th Infantry Regiment was a Regular Army formation during this period. Members did not qualify for P.R.N.G. awards unless they were activated Guardsmen.

VERMONT NATIONAL DEFENSE MEDAL; TYPE 1   Elements of the Vermont National Guard were activated in the 1951 call up of eight National Guard divisions. Two divisions, including the Vermont units, were sent to Europe. Eligibility dates are June 26, 1950 to July 28, 1954. The Type One was only issued for the Korean period. The reverse of this medal is blank. The Type Two deleted the dates from the obverse and is for Vietnam era service.

DELAWARE NATIONAL GUARD MEDAL   The Delaware National Guard Active Service Medal has a special bar for Korean service. The bar reads: "D.N.G. KOREA".

'LOCAL' & OTHER MEDALS

The custom, so prominent after W.W.1, of towns and cities rewarding their returning servicemen with medals and pins was less common after the Second World War. Perhaps it was a reflection of the attitudes regarding the unpopular, forgotten war in far off Korea that the custom virtually ceased to exist.

These, along with state awards, are not authorized for wear on the uniform while the service member was on Federal service, but depending on local regulations, may be worn by National Guardsmen on state duty.

CHELSEA / NORTH CHELSEA, MASSACHUSETTS KOREA SERVICE MEDAL

This is a bronze medal, with an American Eagle superior to the town seal. The U.N. seal is on the reverse. The red/white/blue ribbon is passed through a cut out in the planchet.

LEOMINSTER, MASSACHUSETTS KOREA SERVICE MEDAL

This is a large broze medal with a map of Korea and the 38th Parallel. The ribbon is red/white/blue. The reverse inscription reads "Presented by the City of Leominster in recognition of service in the Korean War" in six lines.

UNITED DAUGHTERS OF CONFEDERACY KOREA SERVICE MEDAL

This fraternal organization issues war service medals to family members of members of the U.D.C. for each major conflict. All the medals are similar but have different dates and inscriptions. The U.D.C. strongly prefers that only the authorized recipients of these medals possess them.

UNITED DAUGHTERS OF THE CONFEDERACY MEDAL

UNIT COMMENDATIONS

American unit citations are awarded on two levels: the <u>Presidential Unit Citation</u>, awarded by order of the President, and the <u>Meritorious Unit Citation</u>, awarded by the respective service secretary.

The manner of wear and award criterion could differ with the branch of service. All were issued to individuals to wear on the uniform and as streamers for the unit colors. Unit citations are worn permanently by individuals who were assigned during the period for which the award was granted, and by other servicemembers only while actually assigned to the unit. In the Army, unit awards are worn above the right pocket, distinct from individual awards which are worn above the left pocket. The other services wear all awards on the left side but unit awards are below individual decorations in order of precedence, but ahead of foreign awards. The Air Force and Navy/U.S.M.C. unit awards are smaller than those of the Army so that the metal frames will fit in with the other ribbons. The design on the metal frames is a 'V' pattern which is worn with the open end up. Variations of these ribbons are worn by allies to match their uniform styles and regulations. Some are embroidered sew-ons rather than metal-framed pin-ons.

PRESIDENTIAL UNIT CITATIONS

All are awarded in the name of the President of the United States to U.S. and allied units which display "gallantry, determination, and esprit de corps in accomplishing their mission that under extremely difficult or hazardous circumstances set them apart from and above other units participating in the same campaign". The degree of heroism involved is equal to a Distinguished Service Cross/Navy Cross to an individual.

<u>ARMY/AIR FORCE</u>: This was established by Executive Order 9075, February 26, 1942 as the Distinguished Unit Citation. It was redesignated as the Presidential Unit Citation by Executive Order 10694 on January 10, 1957.
The P.U.C. is a blue ribbon with a gilt frame. Multiple awards are signified by oak leaf clusters (Army) or bronze and silver stars (Air Force) as per campaign medals.

<u>NAVY/U.S.M.C.</u> The Navy P.U.C. was established by Executive Order 9050 on February 6, 1942. It is awarded for "outstanding performance in action against an armed enemy of the United States on or after December 7, 1941".

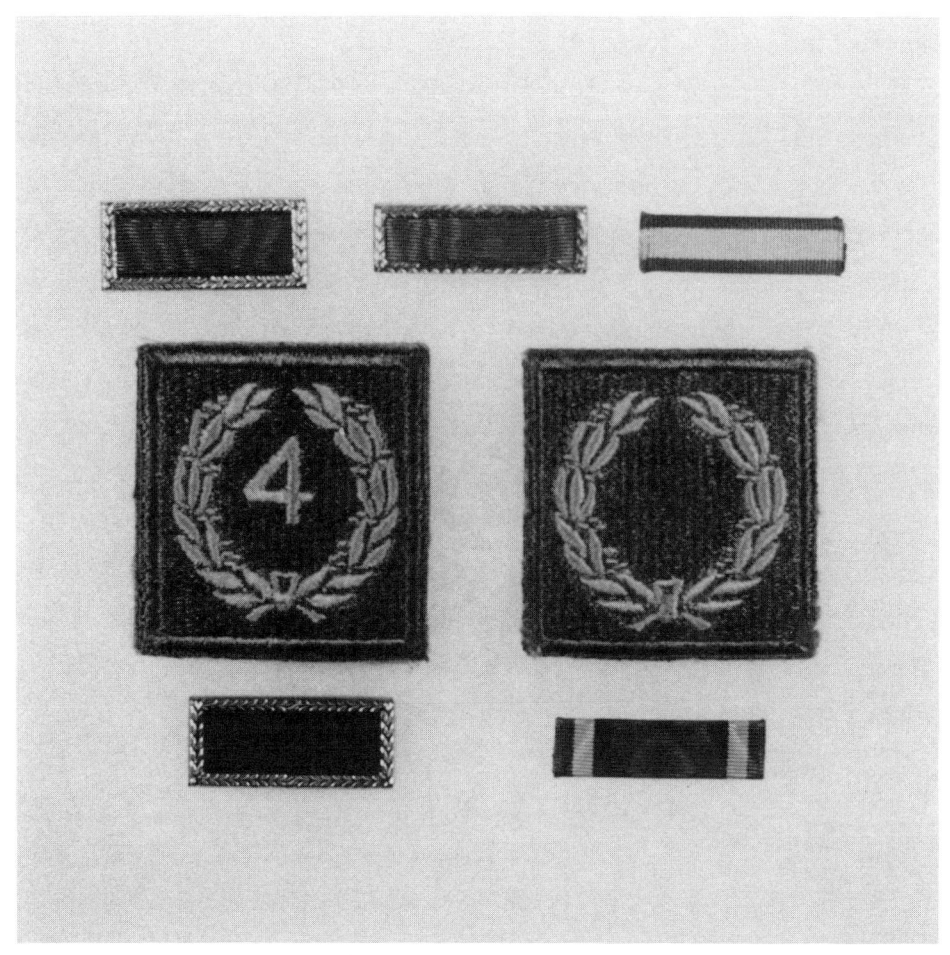

UNIT COMMENDATIONS

ROW 1: PRESIDENTIAL UNIT CITATION; ARMY - AIR FORCE - NAVY.
ROW 2: ARMY MERITORIOUS UNIT CITATION; 4th award; 1 award.
ROW 3: ARMY MERITORIOUS UNIT CITATION; current issue.
NAVAL UNIT CITATION

The Navy P.U.C. has no frame. The ribbon has three horozontal stripes of blue/ yellow/red. Also known at the time of Korea as the Distinguished Unit Citation. The U.S.A.F. and Navy/U.S.M.C. D.U.C.s were renamed on November 3, 1966.

MERITORIOUS UNIT CITATIONS

These are awarded by the service secretary. Award criterion differed with the branch of service. These were only awarded to American units.

ARMY: The Army M.U.C. was an embroidered gold wreath on an olive background and was worn on the lower left sleeve of the service and dress uniforms (Class A and Class B). It is now a gilt framed red ribbon and is worn above the right pocket as per the P.U.C..

Award criteria were strictest for Army units. Six continious months of outstanding combat performance was required. The Army M.U.C. was equal to an individual award of the Legion of Merit.

NAVY/U.S.M.C.: The NAVAL UNIT CITATION was established by the Secretary of the Navy on December 18, 1944. Award is to Naval or Marine units which on or after December 6, 1941 "distinguished itself by heroism in action but not sufficent to warrant the P.U.C.".

The N.U.C. is a green ribbon with blue/gold/red stripes at each end. It could be awarded for combat or non-combat service. This award is equal to an individual award of the Bronze Star Medal.

OAK LEAF CLUSTER

An Oak Leaf Cluster is a device to denote multiple awards to soldiers or airmen. Each additional award is signified by the attachment of a bronze Oak Leaf Cluster device to the ribbon or ribbon bar of the decoration. A silver cluster denotes five awards. The Navy and Marine Corps use bronze and silver stars instead. Oak Leaf Clusters are only used with valor and meritorious service decorations. Only one campaign medal is awarded, multiple tours of duty are not recognized with repeat awards for that campaign. Additional Expeditionary Medals can be awarded but not for service in the same operation or campaign.

In 1991, the U.S. Mint issued a coin to commemorate the thirty-eighth anniversary of the Korean cease-fire. It is available in two grades and can be ordered from the U.S. Mint.

CAMPAIGN STREAMERS

The United States divided the war into a series of related operations each of which formed a distinct phase of the war. A streamer embroidered with the name of the campaign is displayed on the unit colors. Each campaign streamer awarded to a unit entitled members serving in it at the time of award to wear a bronze star on the ribbon or ribbon bar of their Korean Service Medal. Five campaigns were represented by a silver star. The streamers are in the colors of the service medal. Ten campaigns are recognized for Korea. These are:

U.N. DEFENSIVE	27 JUN - 15 SEP 50
U.N. OFFENSIVE	16 SEP - 2 NOV 50
C.C.F. INTERVENTION	3 NOV 50 - 24 JAN 51
FIRST U.N. COUNTEROFFENSIVE	25 JAN - 21 APR 51
C.C.F. SPRING OFFENSIVE	22 APR - 8 JUL 51
U.N. SUMMER - FALL OFFENSIVE	9 JUL - 27 NOV 51
SECOND KOREAN WINTER	28 NOV 51 - 30 APR 52
KOREA SUMMER - FALL 1952	1 MAY - 30 NOV 52
THIRD KOREAN WINTER	1 DEC 52 - 30 APR 53
KOREA SUMMER - FALL 1953	1 MAY - 27 JUL 53

ASSAULT ARROWHEAD

The bronze arrowhead device was worn on the ribbon and ribbon bar of the campaign medal. It was also embroidered onto the campaign streamer in gold thread. The device consists of a small ($\frac{1}{4}$ inch high) bronze arrowhead with the tip pointing up. It is worn to the wearer's right of any campaign stars. It was awarded to recognize participation in the following assault operations:

- AMPHIBIOUS: INCHON 1530-2400 Hours, 15 SEP 50
- AIRBORNE: SUNCHON-SUKCHON 0900-1400 Hours, 20 OCT 50
- AIRBORNE: MUSAN-NI 0900-1000 Hours, 23 MAR 51

However, only one arrowhead is awarded, multiple awards are not made.

In addition, paratroopers who participate in a combat parachute assault or infiltration, wear a small gold star centered on their paratroop badge. Those with two such jumps wear one gold star centered on each outstretched wing of the badge.

Orders and Medals Society of America

PFC Ernest L. West receiving his Medal of Honor from President Eisenhower in 1952.

UNITED STATES OF AMERICA
MEDAL OF HONOR

The Medal of Honor is well known and has been better described elsewhere. Two types were awarded during the Korean War, the Army version and the 1942 Navy version. The U.S.A.F. Medal of Honor wasn't instituted until 1961 so Air Force awardees received the Army medal. A total of 131 Medals of Honor were awarded for Korean actions, of these, 93 were posthumous. 78 went to soldiers, 42 to marines, 7 for sailors (5 to hospital corpsmen serving with the marines as front line medics and two to naval aviators) and the remaining four went to Air Force pilots, all four posthumously.

THE KOREA MoH ROLL   (*Posthumous award)

Name	Unit	Date
*CPL ABRELL, CHARLES G.	2-1 MAR	10 JUN 51
MSG ADAMS, STANLEY T.	E-19 INF	4 FEB 51
CPT BARBER, WILLIAM E.	2-7 MAR	28 NOV - 2 DEC 50
*PFC BARKER, CHARLES H.	K-17 INF	4 JUN 53
*PFC BAUGH, WILLIAM B.	3-1 MAR	29 NOV 50
*HM3c BENFORD, EDWARD C.	ATTD: 1 MARDIV	5 SEP 52
*PFC BENNET, EMORY L.	B-15 INF	24 JUN 51
SGT BLEAK, DAVID B.	MED CO-223 INF	14 JUN 52
*SFC BRITTIN, NELSON V.	I-15 INF	7 MAR 51
*PFC BROWN, MELVIN L.	D-8 ENG BN	4 SEP 50
1LT BURKE, LLOYD L.	G-5 CAV	28 OCT 51
*SFC BURRIS, TONY K.	L-38 INF	8-9 OCT 51
PVT CAFFERATA, HECTOR A. Jr	2-7 MAR	28 NOV 50
*CPL CHAMPAGNE, DAVID B.	1-7 MAR	28 MAY 52
HM3c CHARETTE, WILLIAM R.	ATTD: 1 MARDIV	27 MAR 53
*SGT CHARLETON, CORNELIUS H.	C-24 INF	2 JUN 51
*PFC CHRISTIANSON, STANLEY R.	2-1 MAR	29 SEP 50
*CPL COLLIER, GILBERT G.	F-223 INF	19-20 JUL 53
*CPL COLLIER, JOHN W.	C-27 INF	19 SEP 50
2LT COMMISKEY, HENRY A. Sr	1-1 MAR	20 SEP 50
*CPL CRAIG, GORDON M.	RECON CO, 1 CAV DIV	10 SEP 50
CPL CRUMP, JERRY K.	L-7 INF	6-7 SEP 50
*CPL DAVENPORT, JACK A.	3-5 MAR	21 SEP 50
*MAJ DAVIS, GEORGE A. Jr	334 FS, 4 FG	10 FEB 51
LTC DAVIS, RAYMOND G.	1-7 MAR	1-4 DEC 50

MG DEAN, WILLIAM F.	24 INF DIV	20-21 JUL 50
*CPT DESIDERIO, RIGINALD B.	E-27 INF	27 NOV 50
* HC DEWART, RICHARD D.	ATTD: 1 MARDIV	5 APR 51
CPL DEWEY, DUANE E.	2-5 MAR	16 APR 52
1LT DODD, CARL H.	E-5 INF	30-31 JAN 51
*SFC DUKE, RAY E.	C-21 INF	26 APR 51
*SFC EDWARDS, JUNIOR D.	E-23 INF	2 JAN 51
*CPL ESSEBAGGER, JOHN Jr	A-7 INF	25 APR 51
*LTC FAITH, DON C. Jr	1-32 INF	27 NOV-1 DEC 50 (1)
*PFC GARCIA, FERNANDO LUIS	3-5 MAR	5 SEP 52
*PFC GEORGE, CHARLES	C-179 INF	30 NOV 52
*PFC GILLILAND, CHARLES L.	I-7 INF	25 APR 51
*PFC GOMEZ, EDWARD	2-1 MAR	14 SEP 51
*CPL GOODBLOOD, CLAIR	D-7 INF	24-25 APR 51
*S/SGT GUILLEN, AMBROSIO	2-7 MAR	25 JUL 53
* HC HAMMOND, FRANCIS C.	ATTD: 1 MARDIV	26-27 MAR 53
*CPL HAMMOND, LESTER Jr	A-187 ARCT	14 AUG 52
*MSG HANDRICH. MELVIN O.	C-5 INF	25-26 AUG 50
*PFC HANSON, JACK G.	F-31 INF	7 JUN 51
*1LT HARTELL, LEE R.	A-15 F.A.BN	27 AUG 51
CPT HARVEY, RAYMOND	C-17 INF	9 MAR 51
*1LT HENRY, FREDERICK F.	F-28 INF	1 SEP 50
CPL HERNANDEZ, RODOLPHO P.	G-187 ARCT	31 MAY 51
LT(jg) HUDNER, THOMAS J. Jr	VF-32, USS LEYTE	4 DEC 50
CPL INGMAN, EINER H. Jr	E-17 INF	26 FEB 51
*SGT JECELIN, WILLIAM R.	C-35 INF	19 SEP 50
*SGT JOHNSON, JAMES E.	3-7 MAR	2 DEC 50
*PFC JORDAN, MACK A.	K-21 INF	15 NOV 51
*PVT KANELL, BILLIE G.	I-31 INF	7 SEP 51
*SFC KAUFMAN, LOREN R.	G-9 INF	4-5 SEP 50
*PFC KELLY, JOHN D.	1-7 MAR	28 MAY 52
*PFC KELSO, JACK W.	3-7 MAR	2 OCT 52
S/SGT KENNEMORE, ROBERT S.	2-7 MAR	27-28 NOV 50
* HC KILMER, JOHN D.	ATTD: 1 MARDIV	13 AUG 52
*PFC KNIGHT, NOAH O.	F-7 INF	23-24 NOV 51
*LT(jg) KOELSCH. JOHN K.	U.S.NAVY	3 JUL 51

(1) Supercedes prior award of the Silver Star Medal (1st Oak Leaf Cluster) for gallantry in action, November 27, 1950; HQ, X Corps.

MSG KOUMA, ERNEST R.	A-72 TANK BN	31 AUG-1 SEP 50
*CPT KRZYZOWSKI, EDWARD C.	B-9 INF	31 AUG-4 SEP 51
*2LT KYLE, DARWIN K.	K-7 INF	16 FEB 51
MSG LEE, HUBERT L.	I-23 INF	1 FEB 51
SGT LIBBY, GEORGE D.	C-3 ENG BN	2 AUG 51
*PFC LITTLETON, HERBERT A.	1-7 MAR	22 APR 51
*SGT LONG, CHARLES R.	M-38 INF	12 FEB 51
*1LT LOPEZ, BALDOMERO	1-5 MAR	15 SEP 50
*MAJ LORING, CHARLES R. Jr	80 FBS, 8 FBW	22 NOV 52
*CPL LYELL, WILLIAM F.	F-17 INF	31 AUG 51
*CPL MARTINEZ, BENITO	A-27 INF	6 SEP 52
*SGT MATHEWS, DANIEL P.	2-7 MAR	28 MAR 53
*SGT MAUSERT, FREDERICK W. III	1-7 MAR	12 SEP 51
*1LT McGOVERN, ROBERT M.	A-5 CAV	30 JAN 51
PFC McLAUGHLIN, ALFORD L.	3-5 MAR	4-5 SEP 52
*SGT MENDONCA, LEROY A.	B-7 INF	4 JUL 51
CPT MILLET, LEWIS L.	E-27 INF	7 FEB 51
*1LT MITCHELL, FRANK N.	1-7 MAR	26 NOV 50
CPL MIYAMURA, HIROSHI H.	H-7 INF	24-25 APR 51
SGT MIZE, OLA L.	K-15 INF	10-11 JUN 53
*PFC MONEGAN, WALTER C. Jr	2-1 MAR	17 AND 20 SEP 50
*PFC MORELAND, WHITT L.	1-5 MAR	29 MAY 51
*SFC MOYER, DONALD R.	E-35 INF	20 MAY 51
2LT MURPHY, RAYMOND G.	1-5 MAR	3 FEB 51
MAJ MYERS, REGINALD R.	3-1 MAR	29 NOV 50
*PFC OBREGON, EUGENE A.	3-5 MAR	26 SEP 50
2LT O'BRIEN, GEORGE H. Jr	3-7 MAR	27 OCT 52
*PFC OUELLETTE, JOSEPH R.	H-9 INF	31 AUG-3 SEP 50
*LTC PAGE, JOHN U.D.	X CORPS ARTY	29 NOV-10 DEC 50 [1]
*CPL PENDLETON, CHARLES F.	D-15 INF	16-17 JUL 53
*CPL PHILLIPS, LEE H.	2-7 MAR	4 NOV 50
*PFC PILILAAU, HERBERT K.	C-23 INF	17 SEP 51
SGT PITTMAN, JOHN A.	C-23 INF	26 NOV 50
*PFC POMEROY, RALPH E.	E-31 INF	15 OCT 52
*SGT PORTER, DONN F.	G-14 INF	7 SEP 52

[1] LTC Page also received the Navy Cross for the same action.

*SGT POYNTER, JAMES I.	1-7 MAR	4 NOV 50
*2LT RAMER, GEORGE H.	3-7 MAR	12 SEP 51
*CPL RED CLOUD, MITCHELL Jr	E-19 INF	5 NOV 50
*2LT REEM, ROBERT D.	3-7 MAR	6 NOV 50
PFC RODRIGUEZ, JOSEPH C.	F-17 INF	21 MAY 51
CPL ROSSER, RONALD E.	MORTAR CO, 38 INF	12 JAN 52
*CPL SCHOONOVER, DAN D.	A-13 ENG BN	8-10 JUL 53
1LT SCHOWALTER, EDWARD R. Jr	A-31 INF	14 OCT 52
*MAJ SEBILLE, LOUIS J.	67 FBS, 18 FBG	5 AUG 50
*1LT SHEA, RICHARD T. Jr	A-17 INF	6-8 JUL 53
*S/SGT SHUCK, WILLIAM E. Jr	3-7 MAR	3 JUL 52
PFC SIMANEK, ROBERT E.	2-5 MAR	17 AUG 52
*SFC SITMAN, WILLIAM S.	M-23 INF	14 FEB 51
CPT SITTER, CARL L.	3-1 MAR	29-30 NOV 50
*2LT SKINNER, SHERROD E. Jr	2-11 MAR	26 OCT 52
*PFC SMITH, DAVID M.	E-9 INF	1 SEP 50
*CPL SPEICHER, CLIFTON T.	F-223 INF	14 JUN 52
1LT STONE, JAMES L.	E-8 CAV	21-22 NOV 52
*PFC STORY, LUTHER H.	A-9 INF	1 SEP 50
2LT SUDUT, JEROME A.	B-27 INF	12 SEP 51
*PFC THOMPSON, WILLIAM	M-24 INF	6 AUG 50
*SFC TURNER, CHARLES W.	RECON CO, 2 DIV	1 SEP 50
S/SGT VANWINKLE, ARCHIE	1-7 MAR	2 NOV 50
*CPL VITTORI, JOSEPH	2-1 MAR	16-17 SEP 51
*CPT WALMSLEY, JOHN S. Jr	8 BS, 3 BG	14 SEP 51
*S/SGT WATKINS, LEWIS G.	3-7 MAR	7 OCT 52
*MSG WATKINS, TRAVIS E.	H-9 INF	31 AUG-3 SEP 50
PFC WEST, ERNEST L.	L-14 INF	12 OCT 52
MSG WILSON, BENJAMIN F.	I-31 INF	5 JUN 51
T/SGT WILSON, HAROLD E.	3-1 MAR	23-24 APR 51
*PFC WILSON, RICHARD G.	MED CO-187 ARCT	21 OCT 51
*S/SGT WINDRICH, WILLIAM G.	3-5 MAR	1 DEC 50
*PFC WOMACK, BRYANT E.	MED CO-14 INF	12 MAR 52
*PFC YOUNG, ROBERT H.	E-8 CAV	9 OCT 50

Notes on the Korean Medals of Honor:

On July 20, 1950, near Yechon in the Pusan perimeter, a black infantry battalion won America's first ground combat victory in the Korean War. Instrumental in that victory was Lieutenant Charles Bussey. Colonel J. Corley,[1] later commander of the black 24th Infantry, told Lt Bussey that the deed merited the Medal of Honor that he'd been recommended for and that he'd earned a Distinguished Service Cross for another action and "if white, you'd have gotten both".[2] Colonel Corley then stated that he had reduced both awards to the Silver Star and Bronze Star Medals on the basis of Lieutenant Bussey's race. In 1988, the Army agreed to review the flawed official history concerning it's treatment of black troops and to consider the award of the Medal of Honor to Colonel (Retired) Bussey.

In 1985, the Medal of Honor to Sergeant Donn Porter was sold by Sotheby's for $5,000.

Reputable sources indicate that there are about six or seven medals named to Sergeant Pittman. Evidently, Mr Pittman had requested several replacement medals. These medals are of the variety current at the time requested and are also named in the official style current at that time. Four of these are known to be in private collections.

(1) Colonel Corley was once in the Guinness Book of Records for his eight Silver Star Medals.
(2) See "Firefight At Yechon", Bussey, pp 213 - 214. See also "The Forgotten War", Blair, for an accurate account of Yechon.

DISTINGUISHED SERVICE CROSS / NAVY CROSS

These are the second highest American military gallantry awards. While the Navy Cross was intended for sailors and marines, awards of the D.S.C. could be made to the other services and allies. For example, LTG Almond, X Corps commander, presented most of the senior commanders of the 1st Marine Division with the D.S.C. during the November - December 1950 campaign. During the same campaign, a Navy Cross was awarded to an army colonel by the Marine division. The Air Force Cross wasn't instituted until 1962 so Air Force personnel also received the D.S.C..

805 D.S.C. awards were made for the Korean War:

ARMY - 723	ALLIES - 14:	5 - R.O.K.
AIR FORCE - 38		3 - TURKEY
U.S.M.C. - 27		2 - PHILIPPINES
NAVY - 3		2 - UNITED KINGDOM
		1 - BELGIUM
		1 - FRANCE

220 Marines won the Navy Cross, four of these were second awards. This is the highest American valor decoration that can be awarded to a foreigner.

NOTES: For a Korea D.S.C. roll, see "D.S.C. AWARDS FOR THE KOREAN WAR". For details concerning the Navy Cross awards to the Marines, including a roll, refer to "RED BLOOD...PURPLE HEARTS". This book also contains a U.S.M.C. Silver Star roll and information on some recipients and incidents. Details on these books are in the bibliography.

DECORATIONS TO AMERICAN SERVICEMEMBERS

As of 1975, 41,835 valor awards had been made to the U.S. Army, along with 117,315 Purple Heart Medals to the killed and wounded. Comprehensive data concerning American awards is still being gathered. The best readily available sources are the medal rolls and award statistics found in period unit histories.

97 Awards were made to Americans for prisoner of war service.

FROM THE BRITISH COMMONWEALTH

DISTINGUISHED FLYING CROSS, 1st BAR - 2   COL R.A. BERG   U.S.A.F.
　　　　　　　　　　　　　　　　　　　　　　COL L.R. CHASE U.S.A.F.
　　　　　　　　　　　　　　　　　　　　　(original awards were from W.W.2)

DISTINGUISHED FLYING CROSS - U.S.A.F: 8
(R.N.) DISTINGUISHED FLYING MEDAL - U.S.N. : 8   (London Gazette 1955)
(R.N.) DISTINGUISHED SERVICE MEDAL - U.S.N. : 6
　　　　　　　　　　　　　　　　　　　U.S.A.F: 1   CPL C.W. POOLE

FROM THE KINGDOM OF ETHIOPIA

"For meritorious service rendered in support of the Kagnew Battalion"
　　COL E.E. EARNSWORTH
　　COL JOSEPH R. RUSS

(The source didn't specify the awards or name the several other U.S. recipients)

FROM FRANCE

CROIX de LEGION d'HONNEUR - 3   MG W.L. BARRIGER   1953
　　　　　　　　　　　　　　　　　BG W.J. BRADLEY   1953
　　　　　　　　　　　　　　　　　COL DAHLEN, Chester A. 1953

POSTSCRIPT

Via A. Cunningham - Boothe

Remembrance Weekend, November, 1992

At Battersea, London, the Korean Embassy held a 'thank you' party for the British Korean Veteran's Association. Present were these former Royal Northumberland Fusiliers and their guest: from left to right: William Wappett M.M.; Ashley Cunningham - Boothe; Kevin Ingraham; James Thompson M.M. and Joe "Tommo' Thompson. My thanks and regards to these veterans for allowing their junior American cousin the honor of being amongst their ranks that evening.

APPENDIX 1 - AWARD DOCUMENTS

HEADQUARTERS X CORPS
UNITED STATES ARMY

CITATION

AWARD OF THE BRONZE STAR MEDAL

Corporal THOMAS J. CADWELL, US55199274, Artillery, United States Army. Corporal CADWELL, Cannoneer, Battery "A", 780th Field Artillery Battalion, is cited for meritorious service in connection with military operations against an armed enemy in Korea during the period 1 June 1952 to 19 June 1953. Corporal CADWELL performed the duty of cannoneer in an 8-inch Howitzer section with principal duty as operator of a 6-ton truck. At various times he performed other duties in his section as Gunner, No. 1 Man, and ammunition handler. He was often dispatched on logging details that required skill in manuevering his vehicle over hazardous roads. His efficiency and sincere desire to attain superior result in the accomplishment of all assignments added greatly to the success of his unit. The meritorious service rendered by Corporal CADWELL throughout this period reflects great credit on himself and the military service.

Courtesy George B. Harris III

KONINKLIJKE MARINE

DE PRESIDENT VAN DE REPUBLIEK KOREA,

verleent aan: *H. de Jong*

marinenummer: *39362*

de

PRESIDENTIAL UNIT CITATION

als lid van de bemanning van Hr.Ms. *Evertsen*

in de periode 16 juli 1950 tot 27 juli 1953 deel uitmakend van de 7 Vloot der Verenigde Staten van Amerika, ingedeeld bij de strijdkrachten van het Verenigde Naties Commando,

wegens

buitengewoon verdienstelijk optreden ten aanzien van de Republiek Korea.

Voor eensluidend afschrift
G.N. Tack
GEN.MAJ. titulair b.d.
Adjudant in buitengewone dienst,
van Hare Majesteit de Koningin
Voorzitter van de V.O.K.S.

Seoul, 27 juli 1953

w.g. Syngman Rhee

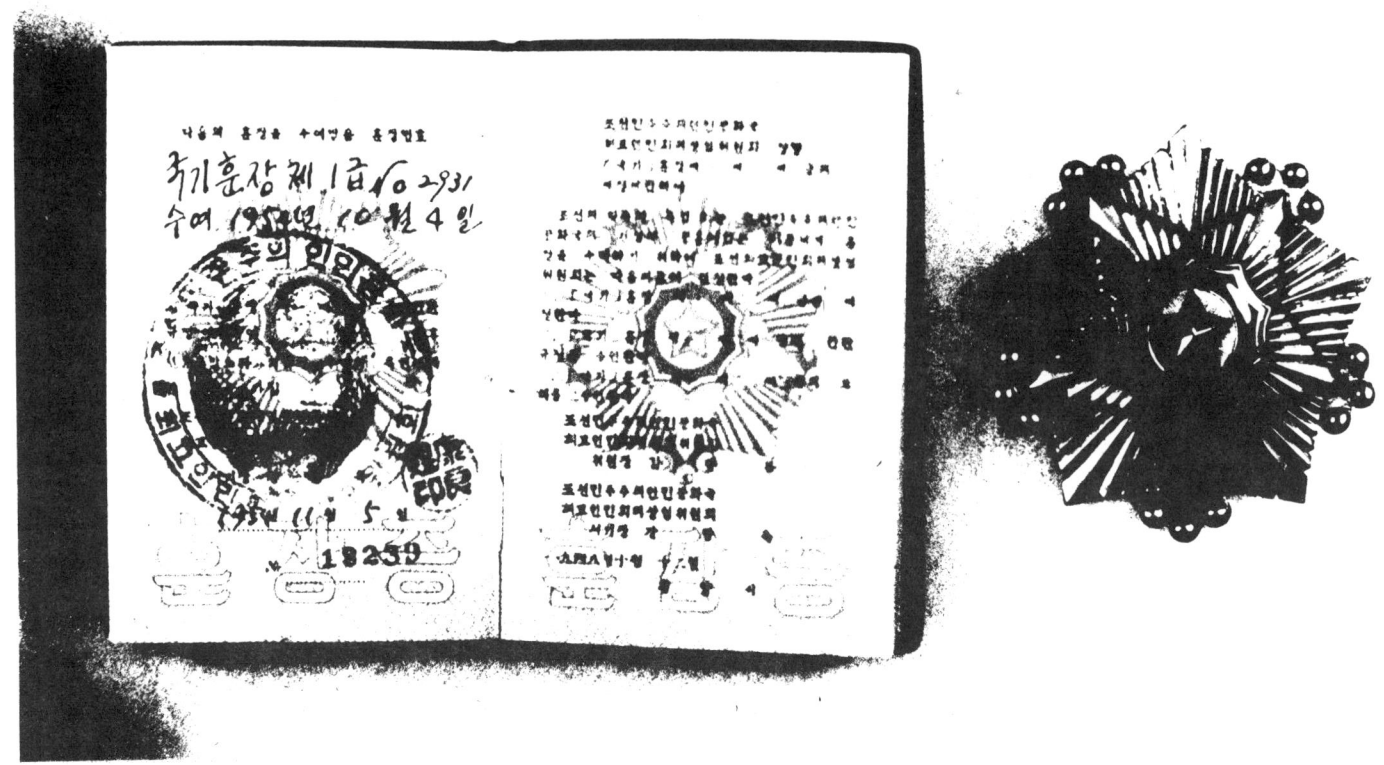

NORTH KOREA - ORDER OF THE BANNER

This, and most high, North Korean awards come with a small, pocket sized booklet similar to that accompanying soviet awards. In it are recorded personal details of the recipient and a brief citation and the serial number of the piece presented. Most of the document is a standard format which describes the priviledges ascribed the bearer as a recipient of this order, such as free use of public transportation. The piece shown here is the 2d Class, Order of the Banner with the matching award booklet.

Award ~ Combat Infantryman Badge

40th INF DIV  **KOREA**

This is to Certify that PRIVATE LOUIE TALLEY US54063008
COMPANY H 224TH INFANTRY REGIMENT
40th Inf Div in Korea, is awarded the Combat Infantryman Badge for active participation in ground combat against an armed enemy of the United States.

Approved: _Joseph P. Cleland_
JOSEPH P CLELAND
MAJOR GENERAL USA
COMMANDING

Hugh P Harris
HUGH P HARRIS
COLONEL INFANTRY
224TH INFANTRY REGIMENT

(Courtesy George B. Harris III)

P.P.C.L.I. Museum

General of the Army Omar Bradley presenting the Honorable Brooke Claxton, Canadian Minister of National Defense, with the American Presidential Unit Citation awarded the Second Battalion, Princess Patricia's Canadian Light Infantry for Kapyong-Ni.

GENERAL ORDERS	DEPARTMENT OF THE ARMY
NO. 52	Washington 25, D.C., 19 July 1951

	Section
BATTLE HONORS—Citation of units	1

☆ ☆ ☆ ☆ ☆

BATTLE HONORS.—As authorized by Executive Order 9396 (Sec. 1, WD Bul. 22, 1943), superseding Executive Order 9075 (Sec. III, WD Bul. 11, 1942), citation of the following units is confirmed in accordance with the provisions of paragraph 2, Army Regulations, 260-15, in the name of the President of the United States as public evidence of deserved honor and distinction. The citation reads as follows:

3D BATTALION, ROYAL AUSTRALIAN REGIMENT

2D BATTALION, PRINCESS PATRICIA'S CANADIAN LIGHT INFANTRY

COMPANY A, 72D HEAVY TANK BATTALION (UNITED STATES)

are cited for extraordinary heroism and outstanding performance of combat duties in action against the armed enemy near Kapyong, Korea, on the 24th and 25th of April 1951. The enemy had broken through the main line of resistance and penetrated to the area north of Kapyong. The units listed above were deployed to stem the assault. Early on the 24th of April, the 3D BATTALION, ROYAL AUSTRALIAN REGIMENT, moved to the right flank of the sector and took up defensive positions north of the Pukhon River. The 2D BATTALION, PRINCESS PATRICIA'S CANADIAN LIGHT INFANTRY, defended in the vicinity of Hill 677 on the left flank. COMPANY A, 72D HEAVY TANK BATTALION, supported all units to the full extent of its capacity and in addition, kept the main roads open and assisted in evacuating the wounded. Troops from a retreating division passed through the sector which enabled enemy troops to infiltrate with the withdrawing forces. The enemy attacked savagely under the clangor of bugles and trumpets. The forward elements were completely surrounded going through the first day and into the second. Again and again the enemy threw waves of troops at the gallant defenders, and many times succeeded in penetrating the outer defense, but each time the courageous, indomitable and determined soldiers repulsed the fanatical attacks. Ammunition ran low and there was no time for food. Critical supplies were dropped by air to the encircled troops, but still they stood their ground in resolute defiance of the enemy. With serene and indefatigable persistence, the gallant soldiers held their defensive positions and took heavy tolls of the enemy. In some instances when the enemy penetrated the defenses, the commanders directed friendly artillery fire on their own positions in repelling the thrusts. Toward the close of the second day, the 25th of April, the enemy break-through had been stopped. The seriousness of the break-through on the central front had been changed from defeat to victory by the gallant stand of these heroic and courageous soldiers. The 3D BATTALION, ROYAL AUSTRALIAN REGIMENT: 2D BATTALION, PRINCESS PATRICIA'S CANADIAN LIGHT INFANTRY, and COMPANY A, 72 HEAVY TANK BATTALION, displayed such gallantry, determination and esprit de corps in accomplishing their mission under extremely difficult and hazardous conditions as to set them apart and above other units participating in the campaign, and by their achievements they have brought distinguished credit on themselves, their homelands, and all freedom-loving nations.

☆ ☆ ☆ ☆ ☆

BY ORDER OF THE SECRETARY OF THE ARMY:

J. LAWTON COLLINS
Chief of Staff, United States Army

OFFICIAL:
WM. E. BERGIN
Major General, USA
Acting The Adjutant General

*By the KING'S Order the name of
Fusilier W. Wappett,
Royal Northumberland Fusiliers,
was published in the London Gazette on
29. June, 1951.
as mentioned in a Despatch for distinguished service.
I am charged to record
His Majesty's high appreciation.*

John Strachey

Secretary of State for War

UNITED KINGDOM - MENTION IN DISPATCHES
The name, regiment and date are printed in red.

Courtesy William Wappett M.M.

BIBLIOGRAPHY

ABBOTT, Peter and THOMAS, Nigel   "THE KOREAN WAR 1950 - 1953"
Men at Arms series No.174   Osprey Publishing   London   1986

ABBOTT, P.E. and TAMPLIN, J.M.A.   "BRITISH GALLANTRY AWARDS"   2d edition
Nimrod, Dix and Co.   London   1981

APPLEMAN, Roy E.   "DISASTER IN KOREA"   Texas A&M University Press   1988

BLATHERWICK, F.J.   CANADIAN ORDERS, DECORATIONS AND MEDALS"   3d edition
Unitrade Press   Toronto   1985

BOYCE, Douglas   "STATE MEDALS FOR WAR SERVICE"   D.B. Enterprises   San Jose   1990

BRYANT, J.G. and COLLINS, D.F.   "A - Z OF MEDALS"   8th edition
Cobra Publications   London   1987

BUSSEY, Charles M.   "FIREFIGHT AT YECHON"   Brassey's   NY   1991

CANADIAN DEPARTMENT OF NATIONAL DEFENSE AWARD REGULATIONS

CUNNINGHAM - BOOTHE, A.   "MARKS OF COURAGE"   Korvet Publishing   Warwickshire   1991

DYKE, Peter   "KOREA 1950 - 1953; UNITED KINGDOM AND COMMONWEALTH PERSONNEL MENTIONED IN DISPATCHES"
Research Publications   Shrewsbury   1989

GASTON, Peter   "KOREA 1950 - 1953; PRISONERS OF WAR, THE BRITISH ARMY"
London Stamp Exchange   London   1976

_____   "THE 38th PARALLEL; THE BRITISH ARMY IN KOREA"
A.D. Hamilton   Glasgow   1976

GLEIM, Albert and HARRIS, George B.   "DISTINGUISHED SERVICE CROSS AWARDS FOR THE KOREAN WAR"
Planchett Press Publication No.39

GLEIM, A. and McDOWELL, C.P.   "THE UNITED NATIONS KOREA SERVICE MEDAL"
Planchett Press Publication No.50   1990

GOULD, Robert J.   "CAMPAIGN MEDALS OF THE BRITISH ARMY 1815 - 1972"
Arms and Armour Press   London   1982

GOULDEN, Joseph   "KOREA, THE UNTOLD STORY OF THE WAR"   Times Books   NY   1982

HARDING, COL E.D. "THE IMJIN ROLL" Goucestershire Regiment 1976

HARRIS, George B. "CATALOG LIST NO.19" privately printed 1986

_____ "UNITED STATES DECORATIONS, AWARDS AND MEDALS" Norlon Publications Margate, Fl 1990

KERRIGAN, Evans "AMERICAN MEDALS AND DECORATIONS" Mallard Press NY 1990

LITHERLAND; JOSLIN; SIMPKIN "BRITISH BATTLES AND MEDALS" Spinks London 1988

MEIJIN; MULDEN; WAGENAAN "ORDERS AND DECORATIONS OF THE NETHERLANDS" 1984

NATIONAL ARMY MUSEUM "PROJECT KOREA; THE BRITISH ARMY IN KOREA 1950 - 1953" National Army Museum London 1989

OLDHAM, G.P., DELAHUNT, B. "ORDERS, DECORATIONS AND MEDALS AWARDED TO NEW ZEALANDERS" privately printed Auckland NZ 1991

OWEN, Colin R. "THE SOUTH AFRICA KOREA MEDAL ROLL" Chimperie Publications Benoni R.S.A. 1982

PHILIPPINE ARMY AWARD REGULATIONS

PRAVAL, K.C. "INDIA'S PARATROOPERS" Thompsen 1974

SALUZZI, Joseph A. "RED BLOOD...PURPLE HEARTS" privately printed NY 1989

SMITH, COL N.C. "HOME BY CHRISTMAS" Mostly Unsung Australia 1990

SOUTH AFRICAN AIR FORCE "PER ASPERA PER ASTRA" S.A.A.F. Golden jubilee souvenir book 1970

SUMMERS, COL Harry "KOREAN WAR ALMANAC" Facts on File NY 1990

THOMAS, LTC P. "41 INDEPENDENT COMMANDO, R.M. KOREA 1950 - 1953" Royal Marines Historical Society Portsmouth 1985, 1990

U.S. GOVERNMENT   "THE CONGRESSIONAL MEDAL OF HONOR
    LIBRARY, THE NAMES, THE DEEDS"
Dell Publishing   NY   1984

VERNON, Sidney B.   "VERNON'S COLLECTORS GUIDE TO ORDERS
    MEDALS AND DECORATIONS"
privately published   1986

WAR HISTORY COMPILATION COMMITTEE   "HISTORY OF THE UNITED
NATIONS FORCES IN THE KOREAN WAR"   Volumes 1 - 6
Republic of Korea Ministry of Defense   1972 - 1976

WILLIAMS, R.D.   "MEDALS TO AUSTRALIA"   3d Ed.   Pocket Book Pubs.
Queensland   1990

ZABARYLO, John M.   "WOUND MEDALS, BADGES AND NEXT OF KIN
    AWARDS OF THE WORLD"
Eagle Enterprises   Edmonton AB   1988

PERIODICALS

ZALOGA, Seven J.   "THE RUSSIANS IN MIG ALLEY"   pp74 - 77
    AIR FORCE MAGAZINE,   February 1991

ORDERS AND MEDALS SOCIETY OF AMERICA   "THE MEDAL COLLECTOR"
and the "JOURNAL OF THE ORDERS AND MEDALS SOCIETY"
(both referenced in the text as "T.M.C.")

GORDELIANOW, Igor   "SOVIET AIR ACES OF THE KOREAN WAR"   pp28
    SMALL AIR FORCES OBSERVER,   January 1993; Vol 17, No 1(65)

RIBBON CHART - 1

UNITED NATIONS

KOREA MEDAL

BELGIUM

WAR VOLUNTEER MEDAL

BELGIUM
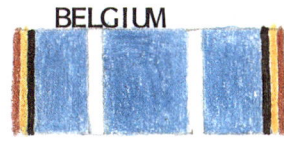
OVERSEAS OPERATIONS MEDAL

LUXEMBOURG

KOREA SERVICE RIBBON

CANADA

KOREA VOLUNTEER SERVICE MEDAL

CHINA; P.R.C.

3 - COMMEMORATIVE MEDAL FOR OPPOSING AMERICA../..VOLUNTEERS IN OPPOSING AMERICA../

COLOMBIA

IRON CROSS / VALOR STAR

COLOMBIA
COLOMBIA INFANTRY BN MEDAL "OLD BALDY" TYPE ONE

COLOMBIA

COLOMBIA INFANTRY BN MEDAL "OLD BALDY" TYPE TWO

COLOMBIA

KOREAN CAMPAIGN MEDAL

DENMARK

JUTLANDIA MEDAL

ETHIOPIA

KOREA MEDAL

FRANCE
COMMEMORATIVE MEDAL FOR U.N. OPERATIONS IN KOREA

FRANCE

CROIX DE GUERRE DE T.O.E.

FRANCE
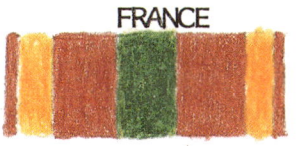
VOLUNTEER COMBATTANT CROSS

INDIA

GENERAL SERVICE MEDAL 1947

INDIA
OVERSEAS SERVICE MEDAL

ITALY

ITALIAN RED CROSS MEDAL FOR WAR ZONE SERVICE

NORTH KOREA

FATHERLAND LIBERATION COMMEMORATION MEDAL

NORTH KOREA

MILITARY MERIT MEDAL

R.O.K.

1950 - 53 WAR SERVICE MEDAL

RIBBON CHART - 2

R.O.K.

TAEGUK D.M.S.M.

R.O.K.

ULCHI D.M.S.M.

R.O.K.

CHUNGMU D.M.S.M.

R.O.K.

WHARANG D.M.S.M.

R.O.K.

STANDARD WOUND MEDAL

R.O.K.

AMBASSADOR OF PEACE MEDAL

R.O.K.
GUERRILLA WAR SERVICE MEDAL

R.O.K.

PRESIDENTIAL UNIT CITATION

NETHERLANDS

CROSS FOR JUSTICE AND FREEDOM

NORWAY

KOREA MEDAL

NORWAY

NORWAY - KOREA FRIENDSHIP SOCIETY MEDAL

PHILIPPINES

KOREA CAMPAIGN MEDAL

PHILIPPINES

PRESIDENTIAL UNIT CITATION

SWEDEN

SWEDISH RED CROSS MEDAL OF MERIT

SWEDEN

SWEDISH RED CROSS SIGN OF MERIT

SOUTH AFRICA

KOREA MEDAL

THAILAND

KOREA MEDAL

UNITED KINGDOM & COMMONWEALTH

KOREA MEDAL

U.S.A.

NATIONAL DEFENSE SERVICE MEDAL

U.S.A.

U.S. MERCHANT MARINE KOREA SERVICE MEDAL

U.S.A.

KOREA SERVICE MEDAL

RIBBON CHART - 3

U.S.A.

ARMED FORCES
EXPEDITIONARY SERVICE
MEDAL

U.S.A.

OCCUPATION SERVICE
(ARMY & NAVY)

U.S.A.

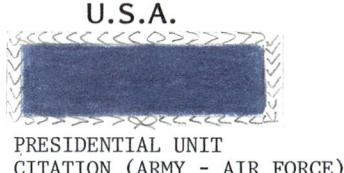

PRESIDENTIAL UNIT
CITATION (ARMY - AIR FORCE)

U.S.A.

PRESIDENTIAL UNIT
CITATION (NAVY - U.S.M.C.)

U.S.A.

MERITORIOUS UNIT
CITATION - ARMY

U.S.A.

NAVY UNIT CITATION

U.S.A.

PUERTO RICO COMBAT
SERVICE MEDAL

U.S.A.

VERMONT NATIONAL DEFENSE
SERVICE MEDAL

U.S.A.

LEOMINSTER / CHELSEA
KOREA SERVICE MEDALS